Creation and the Abrahamic Faiths

Creation and the Abrahamic Faiths

Edited by

Neil Spurway

Cambridge Scholars Publishing

Creation and the Abrahamic Faiths, Edited by Neil Spurway

This book first published 2008. The present binding first published 2008.

Cambridge Scholars Publishing

12 Back Chapman Street, Newcastle upon Tyne, NE6 2XX, UK

British Library Cataloguing in Publication Data
A catalogue record for this book is available from the British Library

Copyright © 2008 by Neil Spurway and contributors

All rights for this book reserved. No part of this book may be reproduced, stored in a retrieval system, or transmitted, in any form or by any means, electronic, mechanical, photocopying, recording or otherwise, without the prior permission of the copyright owner.

ISBN (10): 1-84718-809-5, ISBN (13): 9781847188090

TABLE OF CONTENTS

The Science and Religion Forum vii

Introduction ix
Creation in Three Faiths
Neil Spurway

Chapter One 1
Creation Accounts in the Old Testament
David Wilkinson

Chapter Two 13
The Qur'anic Account of Creation: A Response to David Wilkinson
Basil Altaie

Chapter Three 23
Nothing for a Creator to do: Has Scientific Cosmology Displaced
the Need for a Creator?
Peter Colyer

Chapter Four 29
What Creation Theology? Creation from Nothing v. Creation from Chaos
Sjoerd Bonting

Chapter Five 39
The Dark Backward and Abysm of Time: 19th Century Life Sciences
and Natural Theology
David Knight

Chapter Six 57
Scriptural Geologists and Liberal Anglicans: A Response to David Knight
Neil Spurway

Chapter Seven 65
Creation and the Abrahamic Faiths
Keith Ward

Chapter Eight 81
The Understanding of Creation in Islamic Thought: A Response
to Keith Ward
Basil Altaie

Chapter Nine 91
Judaism and Creation
Dan Cohn-Sherbok

Chapter Ten 103
Creation: The Jewish View
Brian Fox

Chapter Eleven 111
Cosmologies Ancient and Modern: A Response to Dan Cohn-Sherbok
and Brian Fox
John Hedley Brooke

Chapter Twelve 119
Islamic Concepts of Creation and Environmental Sustainability
Mawil Izzi Dien

Chapter Thirteen 135
Can there be a Public Theology of Sustainability? A Response
to Mawil Izzi Dien
Celia Deane-Drummond

Coda 143
Neil Spurway

Index 145

THE SCIENCE AND RELIGION FORUM: SEEKING BOTH INTELLIGIBILITY AND MEANING

Growing out of informal discussion meetings which began in 1972, around the key figure of Revd Dr Arthur Peacocke, the Science And Religion Forum was formally inaugurated in 1975. Its stated purpose was to enable further discussion of the issues which arise in the interaction between scientific understanding and religious thought. These issues, together with the social and ethical decisions demanded by scientific advances, have remained the subject of the Forum's meetings since that date.

In 2005 the Forum merged with the Christ and the Cosmos Initiative. This had been founded by the Revd Bill Gowland, a past President of the Methodist Conference, with the intention of bringing the latest knowledge of scientific thinking within the orbit of the enquiring layperson.

Thus enlarged, the Forum is open to all who are concerned to relate established scientific knowledge and methodology to religious faith and practice. Focusing its broader objectives, it seeks particularly to:
1) encourage scientists with limited knowledge of religion, and religious people with limited knowledge of science, to enhance their comprehension of one another's positions
2) provide an interface between academics, active in science-religion work, and public communicators – notably teachers, clerics, and those training future members of these professions.
At every point, the Forum strives to extend recognition that science and religion, properly understood, are not antagonists, but complementary in the quest for truth.

The Forum holds a regular annual conference, plus occasional smaller *ad hoc* meetings, and publishes a twice-yearly journal, *Reviews in Science and Religion*.

At the date of the present publication the Forum's President is Prof John Hedley Brooke (Oxford) and its Chairman Prof Neil Spurway (Glasgow).

Introduction

Creation in Three Faiths

Neil Spurway

Creation! How we are here. Not *just* us, of course, but bluetits and Hereford cattle and humpback whales … and oak trees and cabbages and mildew and *E. coli* … and granite and sandstone and deserts and mountains and moons and suns and nebulae … in fact, the Cosmos – all that is. Not just "Why are we here?", therefore, but "Why is there a 'here' for us to inhabit?". Or, as philosophers are inclined to put the matter, "Why there is something, rather than nothing?"

That is our theme. Inevitably we don't answer the question in a detailed, expository sense – no-one can. A telescope cannot look at itself, and neither can an inhabitant of the Universe say how it came to be. But are there any human beings capable of formulating thoughts who have not at some time asked such questions? One may well suspect, with J.B.S Haldane, that "The Universe is not only queerer than I suppose, but queerer than I *can* suppose". But that does not stop those questions haunting us.

So where shall we turn? To cosmology? It has made huge strides in recent decades, and the concept of an initial event, a "Big Bang", about 14 billion years ago, is now almost universally accepted in the field. But what caused *that*? Most would feel that this is not a question science can answer. So, even though the first two contributors to this book are professional cosmologists and several of the others are well informed about the subject, scientific cosmology is only a background to this book, not its core theme. That theme is the conviction that the truly fundamental explanation for our and the Universe's existence must be a divine Creator – and the specific formulations of that view in the three great monotheistic religions.

These are the faiths which share a common basis in the early history of the Jewish people, and so have been termed the "Abrahamic" faiths. The scriptures of all three include the book of Genesis, and the accounts of creation in its first two chapters. Each faith has added to those accounts –

in the many later books of the Jewish Bible, in the Christian New Testament, and perhaps most radically of all in the Islamic Qur'an. In each faith, too, there have been countless scholarly commentaries on the scriptures. These later developments have moved the expressions of the three faiths considerably apart, and their worship practices have followed and reinforced the dynamics of separation. However, the social and political conditions of the 21st C world make it imperative that every effort should be put into a recovery of understanding between practitioners of the three faiths; thence hopefully a reduction, if not of the differences themselves, at least of the importance placed upon them.

So far, Creation has been referred to in this introductory note as a datable event, but that is by no means the only way the theme must be considered. In the first place to do so would be injudicious, because cosmological thinking might change and the concept of an infinitely long-lasting universe return – perhaps, for instance, with the present one being seen as a single instance in a endless sequence. A truly religious view should not be deterred by this. Quite the opposite, indeed, for the sense of an eternally sustaining deity, upholding creation throughout every moment of its existence and present to every particle of its being, is of the essence for most deep believers. The theological term for this is "immanence", and it is an immanent God, not just one who set the universe going but then withdrew from involvement, whom most people would wish to worship and attempt to serve.

As a particular aspect of service, the citizens of this world are at last waking up to the need to conserve it – to care, not only for one another but for their shared environment, animate and inanimate. To the religious temperament, this is not only a moral imperative but an aspect of worship, a corollary of belief in creation that is as powerful in logic as it is in emotion. So, while the early chapters of the present book are chiefly concerned with belief in God's creative role, as expressed in the myths and metaphors, the scriptures and theologies of the three faiths, several also consider the respective attitudes to environment, and the final chapters focus there. Reassuringly, we find that these attitudes are coming, at least in the current generation, to have a great deal in common.

Structure of the book

The chapters of this book are based on talks given at a conference of the Science and Religion Forum, held in Manchester in Sept 2006. Five main papers were delivered, as plenary lectures, by invited speakers. To all but the first of these there was also a response by a comparably expert commentator with a different viewpoint. There were also a number of rather shorter papers, contributed by participants in the conference and heard by smaller groups. The main papers, the responses, and three of the shorter papers which were judged to contribute substantially to the theme, are collected here – two short papers as stand-alone contributions, the other restructured to constitute a response to the first main paper. This had been given as an open public lecture, so did not receive a pre-arranged, conference-style response at the time. In addition, one intended main paper, which at the last minute could not be given at the conference, is included too. The resultant arithmetic is that two of the chapters are by members of the Jewish faith, three by followers of Islam, and the remaining eight by Christians or representatives of the Christian culture. Overall, this seems a reasonably proportionate reflection of the relative influences of the three Abrahamic faiths in 21st C Britain.

Chapter One

Creation Accounts in the Old Testament

David Wilkinson

Revd Dr David Wilkinson, FRAS, studied in Durham and Cambridge. He has PhDs from Durham in both Theoretical Astrophysics and Systematic Theology. He is a Methodist minister and at the same time Principal of St Johns College, Durham, an Anglican foundation. His many writings in the Science/Religion field include two books: "God, time and Stephen Hawking" (Monarch, 2001) and "Creation" (IVP, 2002)

This lecture, which opened the conference in Sept 2006, was that year's Gowland Lecture. This is an annual lecture in memory of Revd Bill Gowland, another Methodist minister and passionate communicator, who contended that the churches had missed the opportunity offered by the Industrial Revolution, but must not miss that of the Scientific Revolution.

In his Gowland Lecture, David Wilkinson presented the classical Genesis-based view of the creations of the world and of humankind, from the standpoint of a believer who is also a 21st C cosmologist and environmentalist. His account seeks to accord with those of modern-day Jewish and Muslim thinkers as well as of his fellow Christians.

Introduction

It is an immense privilege to be invited to give this annual Gowland lecture. Many of us owe a debt of gratitude to Bill Gowland. As a mentor and a model, he pointed us to the importance of a theology of work through his leadership of Luton Industrial College, the importance of a theology of technology in his *Shaping Tomorrow* project and indeed the importance of a theology of creation in *Christ and the Cosmos*. In all of these different initiatives, Gowland wanted to take the complexity of the modern scientific world seriously. He also wanted to take God seriously, and especially a confidence in God.

It is therefore fitting to be asked to give this lecture on "Creation Accounts in the Old Testament". This is a huge and complex subject, but at heart it is about who God is and confidence in God. Indeed, there are many creation accounts in the Old Testament – or, as many scholars prefer to say, the Hebrew Bible. As well as the much discussed Genesis 1-3, we might add Proverbs 8:22-36, Psalm 8, Psalm 19, Psalm 148, Genesis 9:8-17, Job 38:1-42:17 and Isaiah 40:9-31 as obvious examples.[1] Then there is the way that creation appears in other biblical themes and narratives, in particular the themes of sin, fall and covenant. If that makes our lecture title seem vast, we must remember a further complication. The scriptures do not discuss creation in terms of cosmology for its own sake. Creation is discussed for worship, encouragement, the challenge to holiness, and reassurance. Karl Barth reflected this very clearly in his own theological thinking about creation. He expressed it in terms of the covenant being the "internal basis of creation" (its inner rationale) and of creation being the "external basis of the covenant" (the context within which covenant could be initiated and brought to consummation). By so doing, he attempted to reorientate the discussion away from creation and cosmology to God's relationship with creation and humanity in particular.

Yet the mention of Barth brings one further important dimension to this topic. I come to "Creation Accounts in the Old Testament" from a particular point of view, that is, of a Christian theologian and scientist trained in astrophysics. The scriptures are an extremely rich and diverse source of thinking about creation, and most of us are selective in our reading from our point of view. I am therefore drawn to discuss those passages which resonate both with my interest in science and my Christian faith. I offer this not as a normative way of reading these passages, but as a way of opening up a dialogue with other scholars and faith communities who look to the same passages.

As a Christian theologian, I must acknowledge that the Christian reading of creation passages in the Old Testament has a mixed history. For example, the phrase "let us make humankind" (Genesis 1:26) has sometimes been used in Christian tradition to argue that the Trinitarian understanding of God was there from the beginning. We need to be careful of such an argument, not least because others could argue that in fact the author believed in the multitude of gods of some ancient near east stories rather than one God The temptation is always to read back into the creation accounts, things that are not there in the original authorial intention. Now of course, if one adopts a particular view of the inspiration of Scripture which sees it as having a unity transcending authorial intention, then one can argue for such interpretations being valid. However, at the very least one must acknowledge that this is one of the things that you are bringing to the text. I am therefore, as a Christian theologian, quite committed to reading the scriptures from a perspective of God as Trinity, while stressing that the primary way of understanding "let us" is as "a divine announcement to the heavenly court".

There are even more serious mistakes in the way that Christians have read the Old Testament. The early chapters of Genesis have become a justification for apartheid, the conflict mentality of six day creationism with modern science and the devaluing of the nature and role of women compared to men. However, other Christians have used these very passages to critique racism, creationism and sexism. This is a reminder that our interpretation of these passages is always provisional, often flawed and never should be done in isolation from others who look to these scriptures. It is in this spirit that I offer the following!

I will therefore present a number of major themes which Christian scholars have seen in the creation accounts of the Old Testament. Inevitably these will be illustrated with reference to the early chapters of Genesis.

Theme one: In the beginning God

The first verse of the book of Genesis sets out a clear statement of the sovereignty of God in the creation of the space-time Universe, "In the beginning God created the heavens and the earth" (Gen 1:1). It may be obvious to draw attention to this, but we should not underestimate its importance to the author of this first chapter. Time after time the author returns to this theme in a number of subtle ways.

For example in verse 16 the author writes "God made two great lights – the greater light to govern the day and the lesser light to govern the night." The reference here is to the Sun and the Moon but we need to ask why are they referred to as the greater and lesser lights? Part of the reason seems to be that in other stories of creation in the ancient near east the "Sun" and "Moon" were seen as gods. Here we have theological polemic. By referring to the two great lights, the author is saying that the Sun and Moon are not gods but simply part of the creation of the one God. A similar polemic happens in verse 21, "God created the great sea monsters". This special word for "create" is only used in the creation of the heavens and the earth (Gen 1:1), the creation of humanity (Gen. 1:27) and here in verse 21. We might understand why this word refers to the whole of creation and human beings, but why the great sea monsters? Again in some stories of the ancient near east god has to overcome the great creatures of the sea before creating. The polemic here is to say that even if these great sea creatures exist they are all created by the one God.

Of course scholars debate the nature of polemic and how the author of Genesis 1 uses it. Gunkel in 1895 raised the question of whether Genesis 1 is dependent on other creation stories and many theories have been suggested as to the relationship of the Genesis account to stories in the ancient near east such as the Babylonian creation stories *Enuma Elish* or the *Atrahasis* epic, or Egyptian ideas of creation in such works as *The Teaching of King Merikare*. Some have reduced the Genesis account to a much later work which has simply copied more ancient stories, while others wanting to defend the purity of Genesis as revelation direct from God have emphasised the differences. The truth is probably more complex than either of these standpoints[2]. There are broad parallels between Genesis and the Babylonian stories, such as the separation of heaven and earth, and the schema of creation followed by divine displeasure followed by flood. However, the evidence for direct dependence is weak in all these cases. For example the often quoted parallel that the Babylonian Genesis is written on seven tablets, which parallels the seven days of creation of the Hebrew account, is simply coincidence. The division of the Babylonian story bears no resemblance to its content, or indeed the stages of the story.

Whatever the exact relationship between Genesis 1 and other creation stories, the intention of the author seems clear. The message conveyed by this text is that God is without peer or competitor, he has no rivals in creation. His word is supreme, that is, He speaks and it is done. This theme is picked up in other parts of the scriptures. The book of Isaiah uses creation to ask "Who is like God?" (Isaiah 40:18), the book of Job to speak of the mystery of God (Job 38:4), and various Psalms as an encouragement to worship. As an astrophysicst in the light of the vastness of a Universe 13 billion light years across and containing 100 billion stars in each of 100 billion galaxies, I hear the theological caution of the JB Phillips' book title "Your God is too small".

The sense of God without peer or competitor in creation has led Christians to develop this into an understanding of God's creative work out of nothing. For some, the opening image of a primordial watery chaos over which God's spirit hovered and into which God's word was spoken, leaves open the question as to whether God simply shaped the universe from pre-existing matter, somewhat like an architect imposing order on matter that was ready to hand. This view appeared in Gnostic writers and was, in turn, used for apologetic purposes by Christian apologists such as Justin Martyr who was executed in 165 CE. Indeed there have been some who have argued that "creation out of nothing" is at best ambiguous in Genesis and only came to clear articulation as Christian faith encountered and responded to the questions and challenges of Greek philosophy and Gnostic thought [3].

I think such arguments underestimate the sense of God as sole Creator contained within the creation accounts of the Old Testament[4]. Now of course, the writer of Genesis 1 was much more concerned to proclaim the movement from chaos to order, than to speculate on the absolute origin of things. Nevertheless, it is important to be clear that for the biblical writers there was no significant dualism of God and matter/chaos[5]. The emergence of the doctrine of *creatio ex nihilo* in Christian writers of the second and third centuries such as Theophilus of Antioch, Irenaeus and Tertullian was driven precisely by the concern to maintain the biblical affirmations of the basic goodness of the world and of God's utterly unopposed freedom in creating. All that exists has its source in nothing other God.

Torrance defines the doctrine as:

> "The creation of the universe out of nothing does not mean the creation of the universe out of something that is nothing, but out of nothing at all. It is not created out of anything – it came into being through the absolute fiat of God"s word."[6]

He argues, significantly, that this doctrine and the associated rejection of Gnosticism was important for the development of the natural sciences on account of the affirmation of the fundamental goodness of creation it represents. Creation is distinct *from* God but dependent for its existence *on* God. As such, creation is both to be valued, rather than to be escaped, and free to be investigated rather than worshipped. Along with this, God was not constrained in creating by the limitations of pre-existing matter but could create freely. Thus, to fully understand the God-given order of the universe it was necessary to observe it: that is one of the basic principles of empirical science.

This scriptural understanding of God as sole creator has important things to say not just to the history of science, but also to current scientific discussion. Oxford chemist Peter Atkins promotes the position that God is redundant in modern cosmology:

> "Reductionist science is omnicompetent. Science has never encountered a barrier it has not surmounted or that we can reasonably suppose it has

power to surmount and will in due course be equipped to do so…..Religion has failed, and its failure should be exposed. Science, with its currently successful pursuit of universal competence through the identification of the minimal, the supreme delight of the intellect, should be acknowledged king."[7]

This "conflict" model of science and religion has also tried to enroll Stephen Hawking's view that science may be able to explain the initial conditions of the Universe through a quantum theory of gravity or a "theory of everything". However, as I have argued elsewhere, Hawking's "absence of God" is an attack upon the misguided god of the gaps argument, or indeed a deistic creator who starts the Universe off and then has nothing more to do with the Universe[8]. Hawking does not provide answers to fundamental questions such as the origins of the laws of physics, the purpose of the universe, its order and intelligibility. The Christian theologian will want to affirm Hawking's scientific attempts to explain the first moments of the Universe's history, but will also want to point to questions which are beyond the capacity of science to answer. Without a sense of God as the sole Creator, the Universe will never be understood.

In fact, there are those who suggest that the Big Bang model itself confirms the biblical understanding. Russell suggests that the notion of a historical origination of the universe provides an important corroborative meaning for the logically prior notion of the ontological origination of the universe – the belief that all that exists depends on God regardless of whether or not it had a beginning – although it is not essential to it[9]. The relationship between historical and ontological origin lies in the concept of finitude. The fact that the universe has a finite history is not trivial in the sense that a temporal origination of the universe can provide confirming but not conclusive or essential evidence for ontological origination. If *creatio ex nihilo* was viewed as a hypothesis to understand the Universe then a temporal beginning could be used as confirming evidence alongside other things.

Theme two: God saw that it was good

If modern science depends on the biblical conviction that God as sole Creator of the Universe had freedom in creating, then it also needs a belief that this freedom does not lead to incomprehensible chaos in the Universe. Many historians of science have pointed to the Judaeo-Christian worldview as giving the belief in an inherent order to the natural world, and that this order should be comprehensible[10]. Thus the laws of physics are a reflection of the faithfulness of God in sustaining the Universe and its order.

Genesis 1 is one of the passages which illustrates such an order within creation. God transforms the "formless void" (Gen 1:2) by giving structure through separation and then filling up those structures. Some biblical commentators have also seen a pattern of the number seven which goes beyond the simple seven day structure. For example, there are seven Hebrew words in verse 1, verse 2 has fourteen, and verses 1 to 3 of chapter 2 have thirty-five. The word "God" occurs thirty five times, the word "Earth" occurs twenty one times, and the phrase "God saw that it was good" occurs seven times. Now one does not need to be a great mathematician to see that something very subtle is going on! The order inherent in the chapter communicates that creation has an order to it because of the Creator

A similar message is communicated through the description of the role of Wisdom in creation (Proverbs 8:22-31). Wisdom is before the Universe and fundamental to its creation (v23-29), and Wisdom's relation to the creation is given in terms of an architect (v27-29), a builder (v28) and a ruler (v29). Wisdom is personified and fundamental to the whole creative process, and in particular to ensuring the stability and continuation of the creation. Wisdom is key to the continuous process of fashioning creation into a world which is intelligible, orderly and good. The images of architect and builder give a picture of a well-structured creation. Further, Wisdom rules the chaos of the sea, setting boundaries for it. There is no suggestion of a primeval battle between the waters and God, but simply that the chaos of this world is contained by Wisdom.

This sense of God freely creating the universe in an orderly way not only encouraged the growth of science but also engendered a positive attitude towards the study of nature in theologians otherwise as different as Aquinas and Calvin. Christians need to recapture this positive attitude to science and the creation. While wanting to reject Dawkins' wilder claims about *The God Delusion,* the Christian theologian must be thankful for Dawkins' description of the wonder of evolutionary biology. Too often in the contemporary world church leaders are either fearful or ignorant of science. Yet to be a scientist is affirmed as a calling by the Abrahamic faith traditions, as those who explore the order of the Universe or those who use the order do so because of God.

It is important to note that this sense of God's faithfulness reflected in the order of creation does not give any support for the Intelligent Design movement. This broad umbrella of creationist and anti-reductionist groups has grown in popularity in North America. Some of the arguments regress to "god of the gaps" approaches, but more importantly they ignore one of the most important aspects of the scriptural accounts. This is, the reflection of God in the order of the Universe can only be seen in the dialogue of God's word and his works. None of the biblical accounts suggest that God can be found on the basis of rational argument. When the order of the Universe is discussed it is discussed in the context of a God who speaks and reveals his role as Creator of that order. For example, the heavens declaring the glory of God (Ps 19:1) are held together with the law of the Lord "enlightening the eyes" (Ps 19:8). For the Christian, the New Testament takes this further and says that the Creator God is only fully seen in Jesus Christ. It is telling that there is little mention of Jesus within Intelligent Design.

Theme three: He made the stars also

In case this talk of order gives the impression that the biblical accounts portray God as a boring egghead or divine mathematician who can be blamed for numerous students having to learn calculus, we need to notice another over-riding theme. Alongside the images of lawgiver, king, builder and architect, God is also the great artist in creation.

If we return to Genesis 1 we see creativity and diversity in abundance. The acts of separation (verses 3, 6, 7, 14, 18) give contrasts of heat and cold, oceans and dry land, the brightness of a summer day and the star field of a clear night. These all engage senses and add to our experience of the world as an awe inspiring place. When vegetation and animal life is brought forth it is of various kinds with the ability to reproduce.

As an astrophysicist, I am amused by one of the greatest understatements of the scriptures, "he also made the stars" (v 16)! It is an awe-inspiring by-the-way statement of the creativity of God. I am often asked why God made the Universe so large. After all, if he was only interested in human life, one planet orbiting one star would have been sufficient. Indeed, it might seem that a much slimmed-down natural world could have also sustained human life. However, the Universe contains more stars than grains of sand on the beaches of the world, and the biological environment of the Earth teems with a rich diversity of life. At this point the biblical images of God flinging stars into space give a picture of a divine artist who loves diversity and extravagance in creation. Indeed Psalm 148 uses this extravagance as a source of praise to the Creator. Beyond that, however, modern cosmology is clear that a Universe of the size and age of the one we inhabit was essential for sentient life to have developed, under the existing laws of physics[11].

The past few years have seen new concern about global warming and pollution. Al Gore's *An Inconvenient Truth* and *Live Earth* concerts have been positive that we can turn our abuse around, while other voices such as James Lovelock have been much more pessimistic. While renewed emphasis on care for the environment is to be welcomed, a great deal of the concern remains anthropocentric. The message is often given that we must deal with global warming or else our children will not survive. While this is true, the biblical accounts want us to widen the vision. "The Earth is the Lord's and everything in it" (Psalm 24:1) and we therefore need to protect and sustain the biodiversity of this planet, for to do otherwise is blasphemy. God has given us extravagance, and all that reduces this diversity is a denial of creation. The historian Lynn White, at the American Association for the Advancement of Science in 1967, drew attention to this anthropocentricity:

"We shall continue to have a worsening ecological crisis until we reject the Christian axiom that nature has no reason for existence but to serve man... Both our present science and our present technology are so tinctured with orthodox Christian arrogance towards nature that no solution for our ecological crisis can be expected from them alone."[12]

Thus, Christianity, it is claimed, bears "a huge burden of guilt" for the environmental crisis.

Yet the biblical accounts of creation taken together critique this arrogance towards the natural world. It is striking that the Genesis 1 narrative reaches fulfillment not in the creation of Adam and Eve but in the sabbath day on which "the whole creation glorifies its maker."[13] This provides a perspective on the distinctive role of humans within the created order as that of priests giving voice to creation's praise. That is, resting in, rejoicing in and living out of the sabbath praise of God is regarded here as the very pinnacle of what created reality and human reality in particular is called to. Viewed in this way, we humans are called not just to "use" material reality for our own ends, but to hallow it, to reverence it as God's gift, to work for its flourishing and, in this manner, be viceroys of God's gracious generative sovereignty in God's good world.

This combination of the complex and extravagant diversity within creation with the essential role of human beings does make clear the risk involved in creation. Here the biblical accounts make very clear the effect of human sin upon the land, while at the same time holding out the hope that the God who created this Universe will not stand apart from it, but one day will bring about new creation (Isaiah 65:17-25). It is this combination of risk and hope that motivates and encourages human beings to join with God's purposes in the care and renewal of creation.

Theme four: In the image of God he created them

As we have already seen one can learn much about the biblical accounts by comparing them with other creation accounts in the ancient near east. This is particularly the case when one considers the nature and status of human beings.

In the Babylonian creation story, *Enuma Elish*, human beings are created as the slaves of the gods to look after their every need. In contrast in the Genesis account, God provides food for human beings (Gen 1:29), human beings are made in the image of God (Gen 1:27), they are given responsibility to look after the Earth (Gen 1:26), and in the lovely imagery of chapters 2 and 3 of Genesis human beings walk in the garden with God enjoying intimate relationship and communication.

Of course there has been much debate about the meaning of being made "in the image of God". While some commentators have argued for moral or mental capacities, in recent years studies in the language and context of the ancient Near East have helped us in a deeper understanding of "image". Egyptian and Assyrian texts sometimes describe the king as the image of God, meaning God's representative on earth. Certainly there is a close connection in the Genesis text between "made in the image of God" and God's command to exercise dominion over the natural world (Genesis 1:26-28). To be in the image of God is to be given responsibility. Further, the image of God is not part of the human constitution so much as it is a description of the process of creation that makes human beings different. The image should not be imagined to be a "part" of us, whether our body, our reason or our moral sense. It is not about something we have or something we do, it is about relationship. The Old Testament scholar Claus Westermann writes, "human beings are created in such a way that their very existence is intended to be their relationship to God"[14]. The "image of God" means that we are sufficiently like God that we can have an intimate relationship with him. This special nature of human beings in the biblical accounts is not primarily that we are physically different from the rest of creation, though in many ways we are, but in the fact that God has given us the gift of intimate relationship and responsibility.

This is seen also in Psalm 8 which reflects the themes of the Genesis text. Asking the question of the significance of human beings in the vast cosmos, the psalmist answers in terms of relationship and responsibility as a gift from the initiative of God in the phrases "you made" (v5), "you crowned" (v6) and "you put" (v6).

Thus the meaning of the Universe is not to be found in an impersonal cosmic force, or in a mathematical theory of everything but in a personal God who wants to be in relationship with human beings. We live in a world which often devalues people, if they do not have the right body shape, the right colour of skin, fame, money or power. The biblical accounts of creation define human value in terms of relationship rather than achievement. This insight is important not just for justice in the world, but also in the areas of artificial intelligence and medical science which pose clearly the question "what does it mean to be human?".

As Bill Gowland emphasized, understanding creation is all about understanding the Creator. Among many other things, the biblical accounts present God as sole creator, as the sustainer of order in the Universe, as the source of extravagance and as the seeker of relationship with human beings. You will find this understanding reflected in the Christian doctrine of creation as expounded by Aquinas, Luther and Calvin, but you will also find it, not surprisingly, in other faith communities who look to the same scriptures.

Notes and References

1. For a detailed discussion of these passages see D. Wilkinson, *Creation* (Leicester: IVP, 2002).
2. See for example W. G. Lambert, "A New Look at the Babylonian Background of Genesis," *Journal of Theological Studies* **16** (1965), p. 294; D. T. Tsumura, *The Earth and the Waters in Genesis 1 and 2: A Linguistic Investigation* (Sheffield, Sheffield Academic Press, 1989) pp. 156-57.
3. G. May, "Creatio ex Nihilo: The Doctrine of "Creation out of Nothing" in *Early Christian Thought* (Edinburgh: University of Edinburgh Press, 1994); F. Young, "Creatio ex nihilo: A Context for the Emergence of the Christian Doctrine of Creation", *Scottish Journal of Theology,* **44** (1991) p. 141.
4. See also M. W. Worthing, *God, Creation and Contemporary Physics* (Minneapolis: Augsburg, 1996) p. 76.
5. C. Westermann, *Genesis 1-11* (London: SPCK, 1984) p. 1:109.
6. T.F. Torrance, *The Christian Doctrine of God: One Being, Three Persons* (Edinburgh: T & T Clark, 1996) p. 207.
7. P. Atkins, "The Limitless Power of Science", in *Nature's Imagination,* ed. J. Cornwall (Oxford: Oxford University Press, 1995) pp. 129, 132
8. D. Wilkinson, *God, Time and Stephen Hawking* (Crowborough: Monarch, 2001)
9. R. J. Russell, "T=0: Is it theologically significant?" in *Religion and Science: History, Method, Dialogue,* W. M. Richardson and W. J. Wildman, eds (London: Routledge, 1996) pp. 201-24.

10. R. G. Collingwood, *An Essay on Metaphysics* (Oxford: University Press, 1940); M. B. Foster, "The Christian doctrine of creation and the rise of modern science", *Mind* **43** (1934) pp. 446-468; R. Hooykaas, *Religion and the Rise of Modern Science* (Edinburgh: Scottish Academic Press, 1973); F. Oakley, "Christian theology and the Newtonian science: rise of the concepts of the laws of nature", *Church History* **30** (1961) pp. 433-457; D. Stimson, "Puritanism and the new philosophy in seventeenth century England", *Bull. Inst. Hist. Med.* **3** (1935) pp. 321-334; E. Zilsel, "The genesis of the concept of physical law", *Phys. Rev.* **51** (1942) pp. 245-279.
11. J. D. Barrow, *The Constants of Nature: from alpha to omega* (London: Jonathan Cape, 2002).
12. L. White, "The Historical Roots of our Ecological Crisis", *Science* **155** (1967) p. 1203.
13. D. Fergusson, *The Cosmos and the Creator* (London: SPCK, 1998) p. 17.
14. Westermann, ref. 5, p. 1:158.

Chapter Two

The Qur'anic Account of Creation: A Response to David Wilkinson

M.B. Altaie

Prof Basil Altaie, who obtained his Ph.D. from Manchester University, now holds the Chair of Relativity and Cosmology, Department of Physics, Yarmouk University, Jordan. His main research topics are quantum cosmology and black holes. He has also published expository books in Arabic on relativity, astronomy, and science and religion.

In the latter field, Prof Altaie focuses particularly on the methodology and arguments of the traditional Islamic approach, known as Kalam, in dealing with issues of contemporary debate. This is evidenced in his reactions below, to Dr Wilkinson's talk, where readers will perhaps be struck as much by the difference of flavour between the approaches of the Muslim and the Christian writer as by their differences of substance, appreciable though these are.

Prof Altaie's main focus in this chapter is on the cosmological outlook of the Qur'an – a topic on which he has further things to say in his second contribution to this volume (Chapter 8). However, he closes the present paper with some comments on the Qur'anic view of environmental matters, with Christian and Jewish readers will more readily feel at home; this theme is taken up at greater length by Dr Izzi Dien in Chapter 12.

The question of creation was one of the prime topics considered early on by the Abrahamic faiths. The first two verses of Genesis talk about the creation of the Earth and the Heavens and state that both emerged from water. The Qur'an considers the same topic in a more or less similar way, but with some differences in the details. A reasonable interpretation of these similarities is to think that both the Bible and the Qur'an stem originally from the same source, despite claims that both were infected by the popular myths of the host communities within which they were revealed. One major difference between the Old Testament and the Qur'an lies in the degree of authentication which they respectively enjoy. The Old Testament is a 'library' much older than the single-source Qur'an, which was dictated by the Prophet Mohammad. For this reason Muslims think that the Qur'an is more authentic, and therefore more reliable than the Old Testament.

Creation is mentioned in the Qur'an in numerous verses, and in them, as in the Old Testament, we notice that the intention is to draw humankind's attention to the order and perfection of creation, the greatness of the creator and his oneness. The goal is to get to know that behind this creation there exists a God who wants us to know him.

In response to David Wilkinson I will discuss the views that can be construed from the Qur'an about creation, development, and the fate of the universe in particular.

The Heavens

The Qur'an talks about the Earth and Heavens in numerous verses, 310 in total. Generally, the term "Heaven" is used to describe the vast space above the Earth extending to infinity. The term "Heaven" (singular) is used 120 times and the term "Heavens" (plural) 190 times.

The Qur'anic description of the Heaven and Heavens appears, at first glance, somewhat vague. This is mainly caused by the many confusing facets to the usage of these words. In a number of verses the Qur'an speaks of *seven* stacked heavens one above another, for example:

> It is He who has created seven heavens, one above the other. You can see no flaw in the creation of the Beneficent God. Look again. Can you see faults? (67:03)[1].

From another set of verses we understand that the heaven is a well-guarded roof. For instance: "And We have made the heaven a guarded canopy and (yet) they turn aside from its portents." (21:32) The Qur'an clearly points to the well structured heaven and indicates that it is built: "What! Are ye the more difficult to create or is it the heaven which Allah hath constructed?" (79:27) This might indicate an influence of the naive view of the public at the time when the Qur'an was revealed, but a close look at other related verses shows that this is not the case.

As Dr Wilkinson says, the scriptures are an extremely rich and diverse source of thinking about creation and most of us read them selectively from our own point of view. However, it should be stressed that the reading should be comprehensive enough to cover all the related texts. This is necessary in order to achieve an accurate overview of the topics concerned.

In an extensive recent study of the terms "Heaven" and "Heavens" in the Qur'an, it is shown that that the Qur'an did not describes the heavens as they were previously understood by the Greeks[2]. As is the case with many other terms, "Heaven" and "Heavens" are contextual and the correct meanings cannot be realized unless the context in which the terms are stated is fully considered.

I can identify three major meanings for the term "Heaven":
1. The Earth's atmosphere
2. Our arm of our galaxy
3. The whole universe.

Of the seven, the first is the lowest or nearby Heaven (*Sama' al-Dunya*) and the rest are the upper or high heavens. The *lowest Heaven* is cited three times and it is always mentioned in conjunction with the planets: "We have adorned the lowest heaven with adorning planets". (37:006)

This verse is important to refute the claim that the seven heavens referred to in the Qur'an are the seven heavenly spheres of the planets suggested by the early Greeks. The five historically recognized planets (Mercury, Venus, Mars, Jupiter, and Saturn) along with the Moon and the Sun were actually well known to the Arabs long before the revelation of the Qur'an. Being in contact with the Greeks and the Romans through Syria, those Arabs had certainly understood these celestial objects to be stacked in the concentric spheres of Aristotle or the later more sophisticated model of Ptolemy. So, when the Qur'an describes these planets as some coronation of the *lower* Heaven in particular, it would be inadequate to conclude that the seven Heavens meant by the Qur'an are those spheres of Aristotle. Rather, they are: "A revelation from Him Who created the Earth and the upper high heavens." (20:04)

The lower heaven is the one containing the air and the clouds. In this sense it is what we call "the sky" from which the Qur'an tells us that rain comes. But the lower heaven is more than that since it includes the planets and the stars.

Another allusion to it is as *"The heaven of the Zodiacal Signs"*. (85:001). This suggests that the lower heaven is meant to be the Earth's atmosphere plus at least the solar system and the nearby collection of the stars, including the constellations which are in fact situated within the spiral arm of the Milky Way to which we belong. But this interpretation of the verses should not limit the scope of the Heaven to the Galaxy, for many other verses point to a wider scope. For example, speaking about "extending the Heaven", as it happens to be in another verse would point to an even larger space. This point will be further discussed below.

There remains the dilemma of there being a total of seven Heavens. This is a problem that I find irresolvable within the scope of our contemporary astronomical knowledge. If one assumes that the Qur'an has a human source, one will ascribe this uncertainty to its author's lack of knowledge. But then the question will arise why this term has been repeated 190 times unless it was fully meaningful to the author? If Mohammad was the author of the Qur'an, and if he was not properly informed about this term, he would surely not have repeated the term so many times. For this reason I would rather suggest that the more realistic view assumes that the Qur'an is actually authored by God. The difficulty lies in the fact that no reasonable model is available which fits this term. Therefore, I would consider this term, the "seven Heavens", to be radically obscure. However, such a consideration will by no means affect our interpretations of the other Qur'anic verses considered in this paper.

Creation of the universe

Sometime the Qur'an is understood to indicate that Heaven was originally created out of nothing, since the word "create" in Arabic would normally be taken to mean "find out of nothing". Nevertheless, this suggestion is controversial.[3]

In 29 verses mention of the Heavens is coupled with that of Earth, with the term Heavens preceding the term Earth, a point that the early commentators on the Qur'an took to indicate the temporal order of creation.

> Behold! in the creation of the Heavens and the Earth, and the alternation of Night and Day, there are indeed Signs for men of understanding. (3:190)

We also read:

> Praise be to Allah, Who created the Heavens and the Earth, and made the Darkness and the Light. Yet those who reject Faith hold (others) as equal with their Guardian-Lord. (2:190).

However, conjoining two more verses we find that the seven Heavens were made out of an original one which was in the state of smoke:

> It is He who created everything on earth for you. Then, directing His order towards the Heaven, He turned it into seven heavens. He has knowledge of all things. (2: 29)

And:

> He established His dominance over the sky, which (for that time) was like smoke. Then He told the heavens and the earth, "Take your shape either willingly or by force" They said," willingly we obey". He formed the seven heavens in two days and revealed to each one its task. He decked the sky above the earth with torches and protected it from (intruders). Such is the design of the Majestic and All-knowing God. (41:11-12)

The 'smoke' that is mentioned in this verse might be presumed to mean a hot gas or mixture of hot gases. (The word 'gas' itself does not exist in the original Arabic).

The verse may be understood to indicate that the seven Heavens were structured after the creation of the original heaven and the Earth. Some authors[4] claim that the Qur'an states that the Earth was created before the heavens, but this is a misinterpretation of the Arabic. In fact even early commentators of the Qur'an have denounced such a flawed understanding and have pointed out that the verse does not necessarily stipulate temporal ordering of creation[5]. Nowhere in the Qur'an is there any explicit indication that Earth was created *before* heaven. On the contrary, the repeated references to heaven and the heavens, prior to any mention of the Earth would appear to indicate that it was heaven which was created first. The Qur'an also clearly states that the heavens and the Earth were both attached (joined) together but was later detached.

> Do not the Unbelievers see that the heavens and the Earth were joined together (as one unit of Creation), before We clove them asunder? We made from water every living thing. Will they not then believe? (21:30)

This verse may well be compared with the description given in Genesis:

> In the beginning God created the heavens and the Earth. Now the Earth was formless and empty. Darkness was on the surface of the deep. God's Spirit was hovering over the surface of the waters. God said, "Let there be an expanse in the middle of the waters, and let it divide the waters from the waters."
> God made the expanse, and divided the waters which were under the expanse from the waters which were above the expanse; and it was so. God called the expanse "sky." There was evening and there was morning, a second day.

God said, "Let the waters under the sky be gathered together to one place, and let the dry land appear;" and it was so. God called the dry land "Earth," and the gathering together of the waters he called "seas." God saw that it was good. (Genesis 1: 1-10)

It might seem that the Qur'an is telling the same story as the Old Testament, since the Qur'an has indicated the union between the Heavens and the Earth. However, we have to look through the whole context of creation of the Heavens and remember that the Qur'an has indicated a hot origin for the Heavens as these were generated from a single Heaven which was in a state of smoke (41:11-12). Here I have to stress again the fact that smoke in Arabic is a hot gas emanating from fire and perhaps containing dust.

The Old Testament's story of creating the Heavens and Earth might have been influenced by the earlier Babylonian literature which tells us that in the beginning there were only vast waters out of which Earth and Heaven originated. Moreover, the Qur'an properly tells that all living creatures were made from water.

Development of the universe

The Qur'an affirms that God created the heaven with power and he is extending it. We read: "We constructed the sky with our hands, and we will continue to expand it." (51:047)

The "extension" was understood by early commentaries on the Qur'an as being an extension of the sides of the heavens.[6] Thus the Qur'an talks about an "extension" of the initially-constructed heaven. From the exact Arabic wording we understand that the extension is meant to take place through adding more construction from within, in addition to extending space. This would mean that there is a continuous creation of matter and energy within the universe. The alternative word will entail expanding the construction which already exists not by adding more construction from within, but by increasing the separations between the constituents of the heaven. However, these alternatives are not yet observationally testable by modern cosmology despite the fact that both alternatives are theoretically possible. The dominant contemporary view is that the universe is expanding not extending, in the sense implied above.

The fate of the universe

Two verses of the Qur'an explicitly state that the heavens will ultimately collapse into a state similar to the initial one.

> The day when We roll up heaven like the rolling up of the scroll of writings. As We began the first creation, We shall reproduce it. A promise (binding) on Us. We shall bring it about. (21:104)

This verse points to the end phase of the universe. It may be taken to indicate a cyclic universe. Combined with the verse talking earlier about expansion it gives us the picture that the universe once created goes on to grow larger and larger until the time comes when it gets folded up to a final phase by which it reverts to a state similar to that in which it started. This may be taken to indicate a sort of cyclic universe. The strange thing is that the verse describes the collapse of the universe as if it is a sheet of flat paper which will be rolled up onto itself. In this sense the universe may end up in a big crunch, a reverse state to the big bang. This suggestion of rolling up the universe like rolling a sheet of paper is new to the scientific concepts of cosmology. Recent observations of the cosmic microwave background indicate that the spatial section of the universe is flat[7]. According to the prevailing theory of cosmic structure represented by the Friedmann models, such a universe should not experience any final collapse phase but instead will go on expanding for ever. The idea that a flat universe may collapse provoked us to investigate this possibility. The results of research work done under my supervision confirm such a possibility with the condition that the universe be driven by a time-dependent cosmological constant. The results also show that such a universe would be cyclic.[8]

> No just value have they made of Allah, such as is due to Him: on the Day of Judgment the whole of the Earth will be but His handful, and the heavens will be rolled up in His right hand: Glory to Him! High is He above the Partners they attribute to Him!" (39:67)

The fate of the Sun

The Qur'an states the final fate of the Sun too. The Sun is said to experience major collapse for its final fate. We read: "When the Sun is folded up (made to collapse)." (81:01). During this time the heaven will exhibit bizarre appearance; it will turn red (55:37), the stars will look fuzzy (81:02) and oceans will catch fire (81:06). Such a description can be easily accommodated within the scope of contemporary astrophysical expectation for the fate of the Sun. According to the standard model in astrophysics[9] the Sun which is a main sequence star now will continue burning for another 5 billion years after which it will undergo a short-time collapse as the main hydrogen fuel will be exhausted. This collapse will raise the temperature and the pressure inside the core of the Sun. Consequently helium nuclei will fuse in an explosive behaviour which will cause the Sun to become a *Red-Giant*. This Giant will fill up the sky as seen from the Earth. Then in a few thousands of years this giant will collapse into a small hot and faint object called a *White Dwarf*. However, the fate of the Sun is not causally connected with the fate of the universe, though once the Sun goes to its final fate no life will be maintained on earth. Even if the universe were to continue for a long time after life on Earth ceased to exist, there would be no human beings to observe it.

Environment

The environmental policy adopted by the Qur'an is maintained by what I call the principle of "least need". That is to consume as little as is needed to survive, and consequently to pollute as little as possible. This is a general policy that the Qur'an continuously preaches. This may be summarized by the verse

> Use the provisions bestowed upon you by GOD to seek the abode of the Hereafter, without neglecting your share in this world. Be charitable, as GOD has been charitable towards you. Do not keep on corrupting the earth. GOD does not love the corruptors. (28:077).

Similar verses are repeated several times in the Qur'an.

However, I do not see that it is true to say, as in Dr Wilkinson's quoting of Lynn White, that "We shall continue to have a worsening ecological crisis until we reject the Christian axiom that nature has no reason for existence but to serve man..." Is it inescapable that we must spoil nature and spread around pollution if nature is to serve us? To have nature devoted to our service does not necessarily mean that we shall spoil it. The Qur'an was perhaps clearer on this matter; spoiling the environment is done by the acts of people who only care about their needs and selfish luxuries.

> Disasters (Corruption) have spread throughout the land and sea, because of what the people have committed. He thus lets them taste the consequences of some of their works, which they may return (to the right works). (30: 41)

Obviously the taste of some of "their deeds" is what we get out of the hurricanes, typhoons, and repeated tsunamis.

In several verses in the Qur'an, God insistently asks people not to do mischief (corruption) on Earth:

And do not corrupt the earth, after it has been set in order (7: 56)

And O my people! Give just measure and weight, nor withhold from the people the things that are their due: commit not evil in the land with intent to do mischief (11:85).

Obviously mischief when stated in a general context may mean committing moral sins but when it comes in the context of practicing life it means destroying the beautiful creation of God. In this context also verses 7:056, 11:85 of the Qur'an are clearly asking people to refrain from spoiling the environment and to preserve nature.

Summarizing, I would say that much similarity is found between the Bible and the Qur'an in respect to creation because both stem from the same source. The differences may be attributed to the understanding of the authors or the commentators on the Bible.

Notes and References

1. For English renderings of the verses of the Qur'an I have mainly used the famous translation by Abdullah Yusuf Ali. I have also used the translation of M. M. Khan and M. T. Al-Hilali titled "*Interpretation of the meaning of the Noble Qur'an*" published by Al-Birr Foundation, U.K. (1996).
2. M.B. Altaie and M. Al-Zubi, *The meaning of heaven and the heavens in the Qur'an*, to be published (2007).
3. H. Wolfson, *The Philosophy of the Kalam* (Harvard: University Press, 1976) pp. 359-372.
4. R. Carrier, *Cosmology and the Koran: A Response to Muslim Fundamentalists* (2001), http://www.infidels.org/library/modern/richard_carrier/islam.html
5. For example: see the commentary of al-Qurtobi, *Al-Jammi' Li Ahkam al-Qur'an* (Beirut : Dar Ihya' al-Turath al-Arabi, 1985) **17**, p. 52.
6. Ibn Katheer, *Tafseer al-Qur'an al-Adheem*, Rushd bookshop publishers, 2nd edn. (2003) p. 1395.
7. C.L. Bennett et al., "First year WAMP observations: Preliminary maps and basic results", *Astrophysical Journal* **148** (2003) p. 1.
8. M. Daradka, *A collapsing Flat Universe*, M.Sc. thesis, Yarmouk University (2007).
9. A. C. Phillips, *The Physics of Stars*, 2nd edn (New York: John Wiley, 1999).

CHAPTER THREE

NOTHING FOR A CREATOR TO DO: HAS SCIENTIFIC COSMOLOGY DISPLACED THE NEED FOR A CREATOR?

PETER COLYER

Dr Peter Colyer has had a three-part career. He worked first as a research scientist in civil engineering hydraulics. Next he turned to science management, which culminated first as head of the European Science Foundation's scientific networks programme, then as Executive Secretary of Academia Europaea. Finally he took slightly early retirement to pursue Master's and then Doctoral degrees in science and religion at Oxford. He is now a Research Fellow at the Centre for the Study of Christianity and Culture at Regent's Park College.

Dr Colyer's contribution here is based on a Short Paper he gave at the 2006 conference. In it he considers the situation in which theological metaphysics finds itself after the last 25 years of cosmological thinking, and argues that, as result of it, substantial changes are required in the linguistic expression of religious beliefs.

In his introduction to Stephen Hawking's *A Brief History of Time*, Carl Sagan refers provocatively to "a universe with no edge in space, no beginning or end in time, and nothing for a Creator to do."[1] Within the book itself, Hawking asks "What place for a Creator?" if the universe has no spatial or temporal boundaries.[2] In this way Hawking appears to share Sagan's scepticism.

These comments by Sagan and Hawking, to the effect that in their scheme of scientific explanation there is nothing left for a Creator to do, have to be taken seriously. There seems to be a good case for the creator's redundancy if, as Hawking claims, the universe has no spatial edge or temporal beginning. Just as there is no empty "space" into which space-time is expanding, and therefore no boundary to space-time, so also there is no definable "beginning" to space-time. Similarly in the reverse direction, as space-time recedes towards zero, it vanishes into non-existence. Space-time itself is the definition of the universe. (Incidentally, Hawking's well-known closing reference to knowing the mind of God[3] is, in my view, a playful joke at the expense of the believers among his readership, akin to Darwin's oblique references to a creator as a gesture to his Victorian readership rather than an integral part of his argument.)

In everyday understanding creation refers to something that happened at the beginning. Creation means "to make, to bring into existence" and therefore deals with the start of things. This could be in terms of the biblical story in Genesis 1-3, or of a Big Bang, or some other mode of initial creation. In the development of Big Bang theory, science has converged with the Abrahamic faiths at least to the extent that a beginning of the universe can be envisaged, even though it might be described, following the principles of Sagan and Hawking, as a "timeless beginning".

In theological discussion, however, creation is understood in multiple ways. In addition to creation at the beginning, at least two other senses are identified. It is claimed that God, as well as forming the world at the outset, is continuously caring for, sustaining and maintaining it. Indeed, divine support is considered essential to the universe's continued existence at every moment of our experienced time. Additionally it is claimed in the Christian faith that God is making a new creation from renewed human lives and, possibly, from other elements of the existing world. These three aspects of creation may conveniently be referred to by their Latin labels: *creatio ex nihilo*, *creatio continua* and *creatio nova*. In this paper I will examine the claims of Sagan and Hawking in relation to these three meanings of creation.

Creation from Nothing

In relation to *creatio ex nihilo*, it must be accepted that modern cosmological science has enormously changed any possible role for a creator. Astronomical observations, supported by sophisticated mathematics and experimental physics in high-energy particle accelerators which can simulate conditions in the very early moments, appear to have provided a credible model of the beginnings of the universe. The emergence of chemical elements and, much later, of biological life can be explained consistently with the Big Bang model. Everything seems to flow relatively smoothly, without divine intervention, from the enormous quantities of energy present in the Big Bang – though only *relatively* smoothly, as it has been found necessary to introduce an early period of rapid so-called "inflation" to make the calculations work. Thereafter, the abundant wealth and variety of the universe, including biological life on at least one planet, appear to emerge from scientifically explainable processes. But is the Sagan claim of divine redundancy totally convincing? Is it really possible to attribute a Big Bang to a "fluctuation in a quantum vacuum" without any further explanation? It seems unlikely that this could be the last word on the matter. Behind the Big Bang there may be more scientific explanation or a divine will – the need for an explanation still exists.

Reference must also be made to the so-called Anthropic Principle, the remarkable coincidences of apparently independent fundamental physical constants which enable particles and elements to cohere and thus form stars, planets and all physical objects, including humans.[4]

These remarkable coincidences may be regarded as evidence of a planned design, or as pointing to the need for more scientific work on the conditions of the Big Bang. At the very least, the issues raised by the Anthropic Principle demonstrate that the creator cannot yet be dismissed.

These questions still surrounding the Big Bang theory may suggest that the Sagan/ Hawking position is untenable, but let us examine carefully what I have argued. I have suggested that even with all the scientific explanation of the Big Bang there remains a real need for a cause of the cause – but this could be a kind of Aristotelian Prime Mover, a logical back-stop, nothing more. Hawking himself recognises this, noting that the existence of the universe raises the question of why it should exist at all. He asks: "Why does the universe go to all the bother of existing? Is the unified theory so compelling that it brings about its own existence? Or does it need a creator, and, if so, does he (*sic*) have any other effect on the universe?"[5] The Anthropic Principle may point to a designer's intention, or there may be as yet unknown physical reasons for the fundamental constants to have the values they do (which, if discovered, would cause the debate to regress one step further). The maximum that can be claimed on this basis is that a possibility of a creation by a creator still exists – the creator does not necessarily have to be the God of the Abrahamic faiths. Some scientific observers have reduced the need for an intelligent designer to no more than a primeval initiator or "button pusher".[6] Even if the religious claims based on the Anthropic Principle are accepted, the role for a cosmic creator *ex nihilo* is severely reduced. I conclude that a case for *creatio ex nihilo* is still present, but the function of a creator *ex nihilo* is reduced.

Continuous creation

Turning to *creatio continua*, it appears that the role of God as creator/sustainer is even more severely constrained. This role may be regarded as theologically conceptual rather scientifically necessary. The forces involved in the Big Bang seem adequate for the subsequent development of sub-atomic particles, chemical elements, stars, planets and life forms. The principle of the conservation of mass/energy appears to suffice for all subsequent developments. The existence of the various species of living things, particularly human beings, could, before the work of Darwin, be regarded as a special area of divine creation, but evolutionary and neo-evolutionary theory has severely questioned that claim. Random variations in genetic replication, the spread of these variations through populations, and the selective processes working through the natural environment, provide the mechanisms for change. The study of living forms leads to awe in face of the variety and richness of the processes, but less place for the role of God.

As far as the distant future is concerned, the situation of living beings cannot be predicted. In a few billions of years the sun will exhaust its supply of fuel, and the earth will become uninhabitable. The available energy will gradually diminish and entropy will increase as the universe moves towards a formless and cold environment close to absolute zero – possibly as a prelude to a reversal of the process towards a Big Crunch. In these future conditions it appears that the forces determining the status of living beings will be physical rather than divine *creatio continua*.

Those who are interested in a genuine interaction of theology and science can no longer derive much strength from a doctrine of creation, whether in its *ex nihilo* or *continua* senses – both senses are grand in scope, but severely reduced in content.

Ironically, the main surviving festival in the Abrahamic faiths relating to the natural world, namely the celebration of Harvest, is increasingly difficult to relate to a scientific view of the world. Harvest rituals express praise to God for the provision of growth and fruitfulness during another year. In times when the availability of food through the year was closely dependent on the previous harvest, such sentiments are easily understood; now that the food market (at least in the developed world) is global and most consumers in developed countries have little awareness of the state of this year's crops in their own or any other locality, the sense of thankfulness for harvest is harder to engender. More fundamentally, harvest liturgies make questionable statements about God's relationship to the fruits of agriculture:

"We plough the fields and scatter the good seed on the land,   but it is fed and watered by God's almighty hand ..."

"All good gifts around us are sent from heaven above ..."

"The cold wind in the winter, the pleasant summer sun, the ripe fruits in the garden, he made them every one ..."

"God our maker will provide for our needs to be supplied ..."

These are poetic statements of course, but are they giving a fair picture of the God of all the world? The succession of seasons is due to the 23½° inclination of the Earth's axis to the plane of the Earth's rotation about the Sun – and four of the planets in our solar system have inclinations between 23° and 29°, so it is unreasonable to attribute this to any particular divine beneficence towards the Earth. Furthermore, the succession of winter cold, gentle rain and summer sun, relates to some limited climatic regions, but not to all. These idyllic descriptions of harvested abundance are appropriate only to a limited region of the Earth. They represent the faith of specially favoured areas, and are inappropriate in marginal zones where the failure of seasonal rains may mean migration and starvation. And theologically, if we praise God for good harvests we must also blame him for droughts and blight. Moreover, praise to God may disguise the need for appreciation to those to whom it is due: the undervalued labour of farmers, processors, transporters and retailers, not to mention the decades of research by agricultural scientists. The liturgy of Harvest shows clearly that beliefs about the God of nature have not kept pace with scientific knowledge.

New creation

The case of the third understanding of creation, *creatio nova*, is different. Here we enter more clearly into human experience and faith. Believers affirm that in their experience God is actively making something new, changing lives, improving the quality of experience, and increasing the prevalence of love in the world. This occurs in the life of the individual, in families and communities, and it spreads to the physical environment. God's *creatio nova* is a personal experience for many people. Sociologists and neurologists may study what is happening in the course of worship or prayer, but such studies need not undermine the reality of religious beliefs, life-changing experiences, the meaning of worship or the value of a supporting community. Sometimes it is implied that if prayer or worship creates particular patterns of brain activity, the exercise must be purely materialistic and the objects of worship are unreal. Would the same be said about the brain patterns produced while listening to music, or driving a car, or playing football? These activities, like religious activities, are conducted in a physical way with observable physical effects, which incorporate a real human experience. *Creatio nova* is the most positive aspect of creation for present-day believers.

My analysis suggests that although a need for belief in *creatio ex nihilo* and *creatio continua* remains, scientific knowledge has had a large negative impact upon the real content of these beliefs. This should be demonstrated in the ways these beliefs are expressed in religious language and liturgy. Much work remains to be done in religious communities to recognise this new reality. In the case of *creatio nova* religious communities have a much better claim to something original, valid, and helpful to society. In this area too new forms of expression are required. In total, serious adjustments are necessary to the ways in which religious communities present their beliefs in God as Creator.

References

1. Carl Sagan, Introduction to Stephen Hawking, *A Brief History of Time* (New York: Bantam, 1988) p. xi.
2. *Ibid*, p. 149.
3. *Ibid*, p. 185.
4. John D. Barrow and Frank J. Tipler, *The Anthropic Cosmological Principle* (Oxford: University Press, 1986); Francesco Bertola and Umberto Curi (eds.), *The Anthropic Principle: Proceedings of the Second Venice Conference on Cosmology and Philosophy* (Cambridge: University Press, 1989).
5. Hawking, *Brief History*, p. 184. Hawking here spoils the quality of his argument by also asking the silly question, "Who made the creator?"
6. Jan Hilgevoord (ed.), *Physics and Our View of the World* (Cambridge: University Press, 1994) p. 286.

CHAPTER FOUR

WHAT CREATION THEOLOGY?
CREATION FROM NOTHING V. CREATION FROM CHAOS

SJOERD L. BONTING

Revd Prof Sjoerd Bonting studied biochemistry in Amsterdam (PhD 1952). He worked in the US for the next 13 years, returned home to the Chair of Biochemstry at Radboud University, Nijmegen (1965-85), and continued as consultant to NASA's preparation of the International Space Station till 1993. While in the US he also studied theology and was ordained into the Episcopal Church. Back in the Netherlands he founded and served four Anglican chaplaincies, and still writes extensively on the theological challenges of modern science. His books include "Chaos Theology" (Novalis, 2002) and "Creation and Double Chaos" (Fortress, 2005).

Here he outlines the thinking of these books, in terms which seem as pertinent to Judaism and Islam as to Christianity. His view is in opposition to that of Wilkinson (Chap 1), and has no consonance with that of Colyer (Chap 3), but the Qur'anic "smoke" (Altaie, Chap 2) could surely be read as an alternative metaphor reaching toward the same idea as Bonting's "chaos"? Nor should Bonting's view be considered recent; an understanding of Genesis in these terms is endorsed by the magisterial Encyclopaedia Judaica,[1] and later chapters of this book will again point to such ideas in ancient Greek as well as mediaeval Jewish thought.

1. Introduction

The three Abrahamic faiths have in common the two creation stories in Gen.1 and 2, which both present creation as occurring from primordial chaos. All non-biblical creation stories also involve some form of initial chaos.[2] The very diverse descriptions of the initial chaos in all these stories indicate that the authors, although asserting the concept, were unable to provide a common definition for it.

What creation theology has been derived from this? In Christianity the commonly held creation theology has been *creatio ex nihilo* (creation out of nothing). This doctrine was formulated by Theophilus of Antioch around 180 AD in his battle against Gnosticism, with its evil demiurge creating the world from evil pre-existing matter.[3]

After its rapid (but rather uncritical) acceptance in the early Christian church, *creatio ex nihilo* was affirmed by the 4th Lateran Council (1215) in connection with the condemnation of the Kathars, and again by the first Vatican Council (1870). However, it is not included in the early creeds and does not seem to have been a topic of discussion at the four great councils of the 4th and 5th centuries and the Council of Trent (1545-63).[4] Consequently, it has not played a role in the formulation of the major Christian doctrines. It was adopted with little discussion by the Reformers. To Luther, *creatio ex nihilo* expressed the dependence of all that is created on God's loving decision.[5] Calvin accepted the doctrine without discussion in his *Institutions*.[6]

In Judaism *creatio ex nihilo* is adopted by some rabbis, but is rejected by others, particularly Maimonides.[7] In the Qur'an it is not directly proposed in any of the 28 suras dealing with creation, but most of them reflect knowledge and imply acceptance of Genesis 1 and 2.[8]

2. Problems of *Creatio ex Nihilo*

Not only does the position of *creatio ex nihilo* in the three Abrahamic faiths seem to be rather shaky, but the doctrine has five major problems:

i) Conceptual

Since we cannot picture absolute nothingness, many theologians assume an "existing" nothing (*nihil ontologicum*) instead of a true nothing (*nihil negativum*). Augustine equates *nihil* with "formless matter, entirely without feature", and Karl Barth and Emil Brunner also hold to an existing nothing, but this is not really different from an initial chaos.[9] I define *nihil* as the complete absence of matter, energy, physical laws, information, structure, and order.

ii) Biblical

The creation accounts in Gen.1 and Gen.2 do not have creation from nothing and Old Testament scholar Claus Westermann states that the abstract concept of creation from *nihil* is foreign to the authors of the creation stories.[10] Gerhard May states: "Nowhere in the New Testament is the doctrine of *creatio ex nihilo* explicitly developed as a cosmological theory."[11]

iii) Scientific

"No physical science, whether classical, quantum mechanical or relativistic, is able to explain the origin of the universe from a *nihil*," concludes Lutheran theologian Mark Worthing from an extensive study, although he remains a believer in *creatio ex nihilo*.[12] He ends his discussion with the statement: "Nothing comes out of nothing."

iv) Theological

A satisfactory theological explanation of creation from nothing has not been supplied. Paul Tillich makes the rather unilluminating statement: "The *nihil* out of which God creates is... the undialectical negation of being."[13] Jürgen Moltmann has made a serious attempt.[14] Combining the ideas of *zimsum* and *shekinah* from the Jewish kabbala (mysticism) with Paul's idea of *kenosis* (Phil. 2:5-8) and the idea of God's self-humiliation in Christ's death on the cross, he states: (1) God withdraws into himself in order to go out of himself in creation; (2) if God is creatively active in the "nothing"which he has ceded and conceded, then the resulting creation still remains in God who has yielded up the initial "nothing" in himself; (3) the initial self-limitation of God, which permits creation, then assumes the glorious, unrestricted boundlessness in which the whole creation is transfigured; (4) in relating initial creation to eschatological creation, Christ's death overcomes the "annihilating nothingness, which persists in sin and death". David Fergusson calls this argumentation "ultimately unconvincing."[15] And I add that a "nothingness that annihilates" can hardly be considered as a true *nihil*.

v) Problem of evil

Creation from *nihil* would imply that God also created evil. This problem has never been resolved in 1800 years of *creatio ex nihilo*, and this is admitted by many contemporary theologians.[16]

3. Defence of *Creatio ex Nihilo*

A thorough defence of the doctrine of *creatio ex nihilo* is rare, except for a recent book by Paul Copan and William L. Craig.[17] Like others, they mention four texts that would support the doctrine: Job 26:7; Rom.4:17; Heb.11:3; 2Macc.7:28. However, a close reading of these texts shows that they fit equally well with creation from chaos. On the scientific problem, Copan and Craig claim that in the big-bang theory the singularity at t = 0 represents "an absolute origin *ex nihilo*", a statement that no cosmologist would agree to. On the theological problem, they do not refer to Moltmann's attempt.[14] The problem of evil that arises from *creatio ex nihilo*, is not at all discussed. Attributing *creatio ex nihilo* as evidence for God's omnipotence, as many defenders of the doctrine do, raises the question whether creation from utter chaos is any less evidence for this. The claim that the doctrine is a philosophical statement, as suggested for instance by Hans Küng,[18] is a fall-back position of little merit: what value has a philosophical statement that conflicts with both biblical and scientific evidence? A scientific theory with so many problems and so little supporting evidence would surely be abandoned.

4. A Revised Creation Theology: Chaos Theology

The shortcomings, set out in sections 2 and 3, of the traditional Christian doctrine of *creatio ex nihilo*, its uncertain status in Judaism and its absence from the Qur'an, seem to me to be a good reason for formulating a revised creation theology. In my "chaos theology" I have formulated a creation theology that does not present any of the five problems associated with the *creatio ex nihilo* doctrine.[19] It offers, moreover, a basis for the other major Christian doctrines of God's action in the world, christology, pneumatology, soteriology and eschatology, and it harmonizes with our modern scientific insights.

Chaos theology can be summarized in four points:

i) Initial creation from primordial chaos

This matches the descriptions in Gen. 1 and 2 and non-biblical creation stories. In cosmology the initial "explosion" would occur in a vacuum with quantum fluctuations.

ii) Continuing creation

The fact that Gen.1-11 is considered to be the full creation story, and Jesus' words ...*God created until now* (Mk.13:19) indicate a continuing creation. This is paralleled in science by cosmic and biological evolution.

iii) Remaining chaos in continuing creation

In 22 places in the Old Testament the "sea" symbolizes a remaining chaos, against which God battles (e.g., Job 26:12; Ps.89:9; Isa.50:2; Jer.51: 36; Nahum 1:4) and which He abolishes on the last day (Rev. 21:1: ... *and the sea was no more*).

iv) Evil emerges from remaining chaos

Physical evil is due to chaotic tectonic forces causing earthquakes and volcanic eruptions; to chaotic behaviour of the Earth's atmosphere causing devastating hurricanes; and to chaotic gene mutations and deregulations causing cancer and other diseases. Moral evil is due to chaotic thinking, as expressed in Paul's words: *I do not understand my own actions. For I do not do what I want, but I do the very thing I hate* (Rom.7:15).

The first three points I consider as biblically founded; the fourth point is my invention. Here evil is not created by God; rather God battles its source until abolishing this on the last day. In my view remaining chaos is morally neutral; it is not only the source of evil, but also permits creative freedom in continuing creation.

Does acceptance of primordial chaos mean reintroduction of Gnostic dualism? I do not think so, because it is not a pre-existent evil matter, but rather a *condition* in the form of the chaos of a vacuum with quantum fluctuations. The first particles, quarks, were not formed until $t = 10^{-35}$ sec after the initial explosion ($t = 0$), protons and neutrons at $t = 10^{-4}$ sec. But where did the primordial chaos in Gen.1 and 2 and the fluctuating vacuum come from? Neither theology, nor science can answer this question; here we get into initial mystery. Cosmology cannot get closer than $t = 10^{-43}$ sec (Planck time) after the initial explosion. The fluctuating vacuum is thought to underly the cosmos throughout time, but nothing definite can be said about $t = 0$, since this is a "singular point" in cosmology. String theory in decades of hard work has not been able to resolve this singularity. Theologically we are handicapped by the very diverse descriptions of primordial chaos in the biblical and non-biblical creation stories, none of which explains its origin. *Creatio ex nihilo* with its *nihil* originally in God, then for creation moved out of God, has its own problem, as Moltmann experienced (section 2, point iv).

5. Applications of chaos theology

In contrast to *creatio ex nihilo*, chaos theology, aided by our scientific insights, can be applied in the development of the major Christian doctrines, as indicated briefly here.

i) God's action in initial creation

Gen.1 and John 1:1-5 have the Logos, God's powerful Word, as the creative agent. In cosmological terms we may say that the Logos provided the energy needed for the kinetic energy of the big bang and later for conversion into the first particles (Philo and Maximilian the Confessor used the term *energeia* for the Logos). There was, however, also information needed in the form of the physical laws and fundamental constants to determine the evolution of cosmos and life. I suggest that this was the role of the Spirit, God's information transmitter (see below, under iv).[20] The interesting point is that this action of the Spirit cannot have occurred until $t = 10^{-35}$ sec, just before the inflation of the early universe and the formation of the quarks. The reason is that quantum theory requires a minimal surface area of one square Planck distance (10^{-35} m) for the insertion of 1 bit of information. At $t = 10^{-35}$ sec the diameter of the early universe was 10^{-30} m, so it could then accept 10 gigabits of information (the equivalent of 10,000 average size books), which would appear to be sufficient for all physical laws and fundamental constants. The joint action of Logos and Spirit fits well with Irenaeus' saying: "The Son and the Spirit are the two hands of God by which he created all things," where Son stands for the pre-existent Christ which is the Logos.

ii) God's action in continuing creation

Divine interference with physical laws or fundamental constants can be excluded, as this would have catastrophic effects. Quantum events or self-organization, as suggested by some, are also unlikely ways. However, the influencing of chaos events appears to be a much more likely way.[21] Living organisms, Earth's atmosphere, solar sytems and others are "non-linear systems". This means that in the course of time such a system reaches a fork in the road, where it begins to oscillate between the two legs of the fork. Since there is no energy difference between the two legs, we cannot predict how the system will travel. The system becomes "chaotic", unpredictable. However, a very minute influence, such as the introduction of a single bit of information, can steer the system without violating any physical law. The event will, however, be so rapid and require so little energy (for the introduction of one bit of information) that it will be undetectable for us, except for its effects.

iii) The cosmic Christ and reconciliation

Over the centuries popular Christian belief has regrettably narrowed down salvation to us humans, with blithe disregard for the fate of all other creatures.[22] Yet, Paul and John already recognized in Jesus the *cosmic Christ,* in whom God was reconciling the world (Gk *kosmos*) to himself (2 Cor.5:19; Jn.3:17). The idea of Jesus as the cosmic Christ is supported by our knowledge of cosmic evolution. The hydrogen, resulting from the big bang, condensed into stars, which through nuclear fusion produced the heavier chemical elements. After exhausting their nuclear fuel, these stars turned into supernovae, which exploded and ejected these elements into the interstellar space as "cosmic dust". Eventually, Sun and Earth were formed through accretion of these elements from the cosmic dust. All living beings, including humans, are formed from these elements through the uptake of food. As it is said: "We are made of stardust". This means that we humans are part of, are united with the entire cosmos. The human Jesus also shares in this cosmic union, and thus through the incarnation he becomes the cosmic Christ. This has decisive consequences for our understanding of his reconciling work. In chaos theology I hold that in continuing creation God battles remaining chaos, for 13.7 billion years already, in which humans existed only during the last 200,000 years. So this is not only a human predicament, but a cosmic drama (Rom. 8:22). In this ongoing battle God is not merely redeeming humans, but the entire cosmos through the cosmic Christ. However, humans have to say "Yes" or "No" to this. This theology of salvation integrates crucifixion, incarnation and resurrection, places reconciliation in the continuing creation on the way to its fulfillment on the last day, and does not picture God as a captive of his own justice. Crucial for us humans is our acceptance of the freely offered reconciliation in and through faith.

iv) Action of the Spirit

From a survey of the numerous biblical references to the Spirit (195 in the Old Testament, 302 in the New) I have concluded that the diverse activities of the Spirit can be brought together under the heading of "communication" or "information transfer".[20] This fits the crucial role I assigned to the Spirit in the initial creation, that of inserting the physical laws and fundamental constants in the early universe (see i above). It also fits a role for the Spirit in transferring the information for influencing chaos events during continuing creation (see ii above). And under v below I suggest a role for the Spirit in the eschatological event. The Spirit's more familiar functions as Life-giver, Unifier, Revealer, Sanctifier and Advocate can also be seen in terms of information transfer, communication. These considerations lead to a broader and deeper pneumatology than is provided in traditional theology.

v) Eschatology

Here we encounter a radical clash between the somber cosmological predictions and the hopeful biblical message.[23] A possible cosmological scenario predicts that in some 24 billion years the universe will go to complete degradation, the so-called "big rip". Galactic clusters are drifting apart ever faster, in the final billion years galaxies and solar systems will break up, in the final 30 min stars and planets will disintegrate, in the final split-second molecules and atoms will tear apart and their constituent particles will "evaporate", leaving only a cold, dark, lifeless and matterless cloud of photons, the vacuum with quantum fluctuations. The alternative (less likely) cosmological scenario of the "big crunch" presents no more hospitable prospect. Much earlier than either of these events, some 5 billion years from now, our Sun will have exhausted its nuclear fuel and expand into a "red giant". It will swell until touching the Earth, thereby raising the surface temperature of the Earth to about $1300°$ C, extinguishing all life on Earth.

In the biblical view, however, remaining chaos will be abolished on the last day (... *and the sea was no more*, Rev.21:1) and there will be a new heaven and a new earth. Creation will be perfected.

Why this clash between the two views? The cosmological prediction is based on a "closed universe", which has no energy and information entering it. In the biblical view we have an open universe, where God's energy and information will enter in to bring about the conversion of the present world into a new world. Energy will be brought in by the Logos, now incarnate in Christ. Information in the form of the "physical laws" and "fundamental constants" of the new universe will be inserted by the Spirit. In this case the entry of information does not need to be delayed as in the initial creation, since the then existing universe will have a large dimension.

When will this come about? Jesus said in answer to this question: "Only the Father knows" (Mk.13:32). However, I think that we can safely assume that this will happen before our universe disintegrates and before all life will be destroyed by the Sun turning into a red giant or, much sooner, by ecological catastrophes of our own making. Is this "pie-in-the-sky" thinking? No, for the simple reason that it is unthinkable that God would allow this universe, which he created out of love in a marvelous and extensive process of cosmic and biological evolution, to disintegrate fully before bringing about the new creation. That would amount to declaring the first creation a failure, necessitating a second attempt.

6. Concluding remarks

The three Abrahamic faiths have in common the two creation stories in Gen.1 and 2, which both have creation occurring from primordial chaos. The traditional Christian creation doctrine of *creatio ex nihilo* disregards this aspect of the biblical creation stories. It has, moreover, five serious problems and scant supporting evidence.

In Judaism *creatio ex nihilo* is accepted by some rabbis, but is rejected by others, particularly Maimonides. In the Qur'an it is not found in any of the 28 suras dealing with creation; most of them reflect knowledge and acceptance of the Genesis 1 and 2 stories.

The problems of *creatio ex nihilo* are absent in my more biblical "chaos theology". This revised creation theology might, therefore, provide a bridge between the three Abrahamic faiths and thus further the interfaith dialogue.

Notes and References

1. Cecil Roth and Geoffrey Wigoder, eds, *Encyclopaedia Judaica* (Jerusalem: Keter Publishing, 1972). Article: "Creation and Cosmogony", vol. 5, cols 1061-72.
2. Ellen van Wolde, *Stories of the Beginning* (London: SCM, 1996).
3. Gerhard May, *Creatio ex Nihilo* (Edinburgh: T&T Clark, 1994).
4. Information kindly provided by Prof. Nico Schreurs, Catholic University, Tilburg, the Netherlands.
5. Johannes Schwanke, *Creatio ex Nihilo, Luthers Lehre von der Schöpfung aus dem Nichts in der Groszen Genesis Vorlesung [1535-1545]* (Berlin: Walter de Gruyter, 2004).
6. Information kindly supplied by Dr. Jan Verburg, Doorn, the Netherlands.
7. Rabbi Brian Fox, *Creation, the Jewish view,* this volume, Ch. 10.

8. J.H. Kramers, *De Koran* (Amsterdam: Elsevier, 1969). This annotated Dutch translation of the Qur'an has a concordance, which lists all texts dealing with "creation".
9. Sjoerd L. Bonting, *Creation and Double Chaos* (Minneapolis: Fortress Press, 2005) p. 70.
10. Claus Westermann, *Genesis 1-11: A Commentary* (London: SPCK, 1984) pp. 109, 121.
11. May, ref. 3, p. 26.
12. Mark Worthing, *God, Creation, and Contemporary Physics* (Minneapolis: Fortress Press, 1996) pp. 79-110.
13. Paul Tillich, *Systematic Theology,* vol.1 (Chicago: University of Chicago Press, 1951) p. 188.
14. Jürgen Moltmann, *God in Creation* (San Francisco: Harper, 1991) pp. 86-93.
15. David Fergusson, *The Cosmos and the Creator; An Introduction to the Theology of Creation* (London: SPCK, 1998) p. 25.
16. Sjoerd L. Bonting, ref. 8, pp. 126-141.
17. Paul Copan and William L. Craig, *Creation out of Nothing, A Biblical, Philosophical and Scientific Exploration* (Leicester: Intervarsity Press, 2004).
18. Hans Küng, *Der Anfang aller Dinge* (München: Piper, 2005) p.139.
19. Bonting, ref.8, pp. 94-107.
20. Bonting, Spirit and Creation, *Zygon* **41** (3) (Sept. 2006) pp. 713-26.
21. Bonting, ref.8, pp. 109-122.
22. Bonting, ref.8, pp. 158-172.
23. Bonting, ref.8, pp. 223-236.

CHAPTER FIVE

THE DARK BACKWARD AND ABYSM OF TIME: 19TH CENTURY LIFE SCIENCES AND NATURAL THEOLOGY[1]

DAVID KNIGHT

Prof David Knight (DPhil, Oxford) holds the Emeritus Chair of History and Philosophy of Science and an Honorary Fellowship in the Philosophy Dept, University of Durham. He was President of the British Society for the History of Science, 1994-6. His most recent books are "Science and Spirituality: the Volatile Connection" (Routledge, 2004) and "Public Understanding of Science: a History of Communicating Scientific Ideas" (Routledge, 2006).

The main thrust of the first four chapters has been the juxtaposition of Genesis and Qur'anic accounts of creation with 21st C cosmology. In the 19th C, however, cosmological understanding was insufficient to present a substantial challenge to theological thought. By contrast, biology and geology – geology in its own right, and in its interaction with biology through the fossil record – were moving fast, and stirring minds in powerful yet diverse ways. In this paper, based on a Plenary Lecture at the 2006 conference, Prof Knight gives a picture of that century's intellectual turmoil, much of which represents the initiation of controversies still very active at the start of the 21st C.

It has been said that the average modern science graduate is about as well-prepared for life as the legendary Irish girl arriving at Euston station. A science degree in the twentieth and twenty-first centuries may well not include reflections on ethics, or on the big picture rather than the detailed knowledge which has to be learned. In the nineteenth century, this was not so. Until after 1870, when in the Franco-Prussian War the better-educated nation defeated what had been perceived as the militarily-formidable

French Second Empire, the single-honours degree in science was a novelty in England, and the secular red-brick universities were only just taking off. Except at University College, London, a liberal university education had been expected to include moral and religious instruction. Science was therefore taught in at atmosphere of natural theology; and for a wider readership, it was popularised in this form also, in books, tracts, exhibitions and lectures[2]. God the creator was to be praised for His wisdom and benevolence, and finding out about the world, reading the book of nature, was a religious duty and privilege.

Natural Theology

This interaction worked both ways. In the ancient and medieval world, the Bible was normally read in short passages either liturgically, in the context of worship, or contemplatively and prayerfully as *"lectio divina"*. In either case, there were a variety of ways or levels in which the text might speak to the reader or hearer: perhaps as narrative, as allegory, or as call to action. With the coming of the Renaissance, and the invention of printing, people began to read more widely and less deeply; and the Bible, now much more readily available, was read more and more like a prosy scientific book and less as a collection of stories and poems. A plain meaning clearly expressed was the Enlightenment ideal: imagination and metaphor were as far as possible eschewed in science, for example in Lavoisier's reform of chemistry[3]. This meant that the Bible too was taken very literally: and Creation was seen as more like an event than a process. Archbishop Ussher's date of 4004BC, at the time when the apples would be ripe, was one among a number of computations, but it did acquire the status of Gospel truth even among well-educated Christians. With it went the idea of creation accomplished within six days, literally understood. In the churchyard at St Oswald's church in Durham, there is the grave of Revd George Jackson, who died in 1810, the 5810th year of Freemasonry: he was chaplain to the local Lodge. Adam was of course the first Mason, but presumably did not found his Lodge until four years after the creation of the universe.

The success of Newtonian mechanics in explaining the Solar System and the flight of projectiles, and of artisans and mechanics in making instruments and industrial machinery, boosted the older idea that the cosmos was a giant clock. The chronometers, by 1800 no bigger than a large pocket watch, that transformed navigation were an inspiration for William Paley in 1802 to argue that the world, we, and the other creatures in it were all like watches, carefully designed, in a universe running like clockwork[4]. This was a curiously timeless world, because God did not need to intervene to set it or wind it up; being the best possible, it did not significantly change (Paley's thinking in this not unlike that of his contemporary, the atheist Laplace):

> Yea, the first Morning of Creation wrote
> What the Last Dawn of Reckoning shall read.[5]

Paley was a utilitarian: it was a happy world, but only insofar as it promoted the greatest happiness of the greatest number. Predation provided euthanasia for elderly antelopes (spared the pains of arthritis), and a good meal for wolves and lions. Paley became famous for his clear and readable style. It is fair to say of him that he hoped that readers of *Natural Theology* would go on to his other works of theology and morality: but if they did not, and this particular book was a great publishing success, the God they found was the First Cause of Deism, not a loving father. On these grounds the book found influential critics, who felt that the apologist's task was to make people feel the need for God, not to try to prove his existence; and who might add that the world was imperfect, a gulag, ruined by sin and needing redemption.

Paley's cumulative argument, not a logical proof but a legal one, establishing the goodness and benevolence of God the Designer beyond reasonable doubt, was very impressive and influential. God was not an inscrutable and unpredictable despot, but worked through laws that could be discovered. Charles Darwin at Cambridge enjoyed Paley's book, and his *Origin of Species* (1859) has a similar structure. Neither for Paley nor for Darwin could the life and earth sciences be a matter of logic and experiment such as Lavoisier and Laplace desired. Paley had in his sights David Hume and his *Dialogues Concerning Natural Religion,* where a participant argued that Nature could easily be seen as a cruel stepmother, "pouring forth from her Lap, without Discernment or parental Care, her maim'd and abortive Children.[6] Also prominent in the Scottish Enlightenment was James Hutton, a Deist who saw endless cycles of elevation and erosion, driven by the antagonist powers of heat and water, in a world that, like Aristotle's, was eternal: to the horror of orthodox contemporaries, he found no vestige of a beginning, no prospect of an end.[7] But Hume's cleverness and Hutton's broad sweep and indigestible prose (made more palatable by John Playfair in 1802[8]) had little effect, especially with the coming of the French Revolution in 1789, and its turn to terror in 1793, showing where irreligion led and fuelling suspicion of wide-ranging syntheses.

Paris as the Centre of Things

France was by then, and would be for another generation, the world's centre of scientific excellence right across the board from mathematics to botany and anthropology. And in the hands of Lavoisier and his contemporaries a "second scientific revolution" was in progress, where the grand "systems" of the Enlightenment era were challenged by the demand for rigour. Careful experiment, cautious induction, mathematical and logical deduction, and wariness of hypotheses were demanded: old-fashioned thinkers like J.B.Lamarck were derided by their up-to-date contemporaries, notably Georges Cuvier, Professor at the Museum in Paris and Permanent Secretary of the Academy of Sciences.[9] A Protestant, in his zoological and palaeontological work he was a neo-Aristotelian teleologist, convinced that all the parts of an animal were designed to go together and support its way of life. The skull, jaws, teeth, shoulders, abdomen, legs and feet of herbivores and carnivores for example are very different, and apt for their various purposes. His studies of vertebrates in the Paris zoo and the adjacent museum (where he performed autopsies on those that died) prepared him for work on fossils. In the last years of the eighteenth century, it had finally become clear that "fossils" (meaning originally something dug up) that resembled bones or shells really were the remains of such, even if they had been chemically transformed, perhaps into silica or pyrites. It was also apparent, now that Australia was mapped, Siberia and western North America traversed, and Africa being explored, that some at least of these bones and shells had belonged to creatures now extinct. The bones of mastodons had been found in Ohio, to Thomas Jefferson's excitement; but travellers found none roaming the vast extent of the Louisiana Purchase. As the eminent doctor James Parkinson put it in the title of his book, fossils were the organic remains of a former world: they were dead and gone.[10]

How could God have created creatures like this and then destroyed them, or let them become extinct? Had He perhaps, as Hume had suggested, worked by trial and error? Parkinson's frontispiece to his first volume elegantly presented his solution to the problem. Noah's ark is shown, with the rainbow behind it, and in the foreground on the newly-revealed beach are the remains of animals that had missed the boat. Cuvier's researches showed that this would not do. Napoleon was emulating Augustus, rebuilding Paris as an imperial capital; and the stone quarried in Montmartre turned out to be rich in fossils: the masons were ordered to keep Cuvier informed, and from their finds he was able to reconstruct skeletons. A new Ezekiel, he could almost call extinct creatures back to life; and he became so skilled that he said that from a single bone he could identify an animal. What was then striking was the number of different sorts of similar creatures there had been as one dug deeper. Cuvier recognised that he was not merely confronting one former world, but several. Beneath Paris there was a whole series of distinct faunas.

Like the Vicar of Bray, Cuvier lived in interesting times. He survived the Revolution, the proclamation of the Republic, the Terror, the Directory, the Consulate, Napoleon's coup d'état, the Empire, the Restoration, Napoleon's hundred days, the Restoration again, and the "bourgeois revolution" of 1830 that put Louis Philippe on the throne. His vision of the Earth's history perhaps reflected his own experience. It was constantly interrupted with great catastrophes, destroying most animals. Recently, a frozen mammoth had come to light in melting ice in Siberia; the corpse was hairy, and fresh enough for the dogs to eat. Cuvier reasoned that it must have been quick-frozen: in the twinkling of an eye, Siberia must have changed from an area temperate enough to support herds of elephants into a deep freeze. Cuvier could thus accommodate the series of "revolutions of the globe" within not too long a time-span; thousands of years rather than the millions that some pagan schemes seemed to call for. His essay was translated into English, misleadingly including the word "Theory" in the title, and was a great success; in France there was an edition (somewhat updated) as late as 1877, indicating a longevity comparable to Paley's *Natural Theology* in Britain.[11]

Dinosaurs make their appearance

The Sussex surgeon Gideon Mantell, working on older strata, found bones which he attributed to an enormous reptile resembling an iguana, calling it iguanadon: Cuvier confirmed his discovery, and "the English Cuvier", Richard Owen of the College of Surgeons (who had actually identified an extinct bird, the moa, from a single bone) coined the name dinosaur for this and other species, which Mary Anning was especially good at finding in the cliffs at Lyme Regis.[12] William Buckland had actually discovered the first one, but it was a marine species and didn't attract the same attention as iguanadon. Buckland was a parson's son, an Oxford graduate, who had been ordained and won a college fellowship. He had to give it up on marriage: but, being keen on natural history, took on the Readership in Geology, and began lecturing on fossils to anyone who cared to come. His spirited performances aroused enthusiasm, especially as he managed to reconcile geology with Scripture; and money was found to upgrade his post to a Professorship (though he had nothing like a modern department to preside over). In 1821, he visited the cave at Kirkdale in Yorkshire, which had a great many bones in it. He identified them as those of hyenas and their prey. It was clear that the hyenas had actually lived in the cave, gnawing the bones as he found they still did in the zoo, and defecating just like modern ones: he did some unpleasant experiments in the cause of science. These could not just be odd bones washed there during the Flood, but must have come from animals drowned there and then, in their den. When the waters subsided, Noah's pair of hyenas had fortunately headed for Africa rather than Yorkshire. These bones, the odd boulders found round the country, the deep rounded valleys cut by small streams, and the widespread deposits of gravel were all evidence for the occurrence of the Deluge. Buckland brought Sir Humphry Davy, President of the Royal Society, to see the cave, and reported his discoveries in the Society's *Philosophical Transactions.*[13]

In 1823 Buckland received the Royal Society's highest award, the Copley Medal, for this work – the first geologist to be so honoured. In his address Davy made the point that science has become more exact, and thus must be "kept perfectly distinct" from hypothetical Biblical interpretation:[14]

> In comparing such deductions [as Buckland's] with some brilliant speculations of the last century, it is impossible not to smile at the aberrations of human genius, and to be proud of the progress we have made. ... The more we study nature, the more we obtain proofs of divine power and beneficence; but the laws of nature and the principles of science were to be discovered by labour and industry, and have not been revealed to man; who, with respect to [natural] philosophy, has been left to exert these god-like faculties, by which reason ultimately approaches, in its results, to inspiration.

One of Buckland's pupils was Charles Lyell, who like the best pupils came to disagree with his professor; and Buckland, like the best professors, accepted much of the criticism, and modified his ideas accordingly. In his *Principles of Geology,* Lyell proposed to "attempt to explain the former changes of the Earth's surface, by reference to causes now in operation".[15] His frontispiece, like Parkinson's, made his point in visual language, depicting "the Temple of Serapis at Puzzuoli" near Naples, where organisms and tide lines around the pillars showed that in the last two thousand years they had been half submerged in the sea for a long time, and then raised again well clear of it; and yet were still standing. Long and relatively gentle processes such as we are accustomed to, will, over millions of years, produce great changes: there was no need for Cuvier's and Buckland's postulated catastrophes – they had been prodigal of violence, because they were parsimonious of time. The fossils of Italy, geologically a recent country compared with Britain, showed that some organisms (notably shellfish, the most common fossils) endured right through geological epochs, others appeared and disappeared. He found no mass extinctions such as a catastrophe would produce; and even managed to account for Cuvier's mammoth, as having fallen into a freezing river. The rate of deposition in the estuaries of great rivers like the Nile gave a clue to the hundreds of millions of years of the Earth's history. Charles Darwin on board *HMS Beagle* read the book, and became a convert; but to most geologists Lyell in his denial of progress and insistence on complete uniformity seemed an extremist. He was nevertheless appointed Professor of Geology at King's College, London, the Church of England's answer to UCL: there was no problem for its Episcopal governing body in a long history for the Earth, provided that (with Lyell in the 1830s) one accepted the recent appearance of mankind.

When the Earl of Bridgewater left the huge sum of £8,000 to the Royal Society to publish books demonstrating the wisdom and goodness of God from the latest science, Buckland was an obvious choice to write on geology.[16] He used most of his £1,000 on magnificent illustrations, in the new medium of lithography: showing not only bones and shells, but also dinosaur footprints, bringing these extraordinary "dragons of the prime/ That tare each other in their slime" to the consciousness of his readers.[17] Accepting an abyss of geological time, requiring for its depiction a coloured frontispiece that folds out to more than a metre long to depict the epochs and their characteristic creatures, he saw these aeons as a time of preparation for mankind. Global cooling was the key. In the age of dinosaurs, the Earth would have been uncomfortably hot for humans; but coal measures had already been laid down, so that we could in due course keep warm in the winters of temperate present-day Britain. The dinosaurs were not God's mistakes, buried like a blundering doctor's. God loved them, and had designed them admirably for the state of the world in their era. Where Lyell saw uninterrupted uniformity, however, Buckland saw progress through series of catastrophes like Cuvier's. He was one of the first converts to Louis Agassiz's explanation of those erratic boulders, deep valleys and gravel deposits as the result not of Flood but of Ice Age.

Biblical and Geological Time

He had at Oxford consulted with his friend Edward Bouverie Pusey, the high-church theologian, about the interpretation of the first verse of *Genesis,* and had concluded that it was a theological rather than an historical statement: and that "in the beginning" could include all the vast geological periods before mankind, the Bible's concern, appeared upon the scene. This was more sophisticated than seeing the "days" of *Genesis* as a thousand ages, millions of years each, as various others did; but either solution seemed possible and unthreatening. Geology was not frightening to liberal-minded, well-educated Christians. In due course, gloomy about the small place geology and other sciences occupied in unreformed Oxford, Buckland accepted ecclesiastical preferment as Dean of Westminster, presiding over the nation's shrine; his years as Professor of Geology were unproblematic for this historic post.

The views of Buckland and his Cambridge opposite number, Adam Sedgwick of Trinity College, were very influential in a time when geology was very popular. Sir John Herschel (son of Sir William the great astronomer) was a Cambridge man and one of the gang of four who had forced the university out of antiquated Newton-worship in its prestigious mathematics degree, so that graduates could follow the work of Laplace and his successors. He became the most prominent natural philosopher of the early Victorian period, and in his *Preliminary Discourse* described scientific method: stressing that science was concerned with the world as a going concern, and had no proper interest in the origin of things. He also wrote a poem on the Baconian theme "Man the interpreter of Nature", developing a view like Buckland's:[18]

> Yet what availed, alas! These glorious forms of Creation,
> Forms of transcendent might – Beauty with Majesty joined,
> None to behold, and none to enjoy, and none to interpret?
> Say! Was the WORK wrought out? Say, was the GLORY complete?
> ....
> Man sprang forth at the final behest. His intelligent worship
> Filled up the void which was left. Nature at length had a soul.

But this compromise was not destined to last very long. In 1844 Charles Darwin wrote out a brief version of his theory of evolution (the first to meet, with its idea of natural selection, Herschel's demand that science must involve *verae causae* rather than speculation) for circulation among friends, and to be published if he should die; and the anonymous *Vestiges* provoked a Victorian sensation.[19]

Vestiges was written by the Scottish publisher Robert Chambers, and published secretly and anonymously. In lively style, it proposed cosmic evolution over millions of years, from the fire mist out of which the Sun and planets were formed through a cosmic soup where an electric spark generated life, and on via jerky progressive development to mankind, thoroughly predictable in the mass, properly a subject of science, and perhaps just a stage in a process that would go to produce something better. The book was denounced as atheism, but in fact it was clearly Deistic. Its broad-brush style (based on wide reading rather than exact knowledge) meant that men of science, including T.H.Huxley, found it riddled with errors; whereas clergy deplored its materialism and feared it would lead to immorality. With such bad notices, and such mystery about its author, the book sold very well. Its effect, with that of Lyell, can be seen in that great expression of Victorian doubt, Alfred Tennyson's *In Memoriam,* 1850, with its famous lines:[20]

> [Man] Who trusted God was love indeed
> And love creation's final law –
> Tho' Nature, red in tooth and claw
> With ravine, shriek'd against his creed.

Thus nine years before Darwin published the *Origin of Species,* it was evident that an evolutionary vision might make geological time more challenging to orthodoxy. Clearly, the carnivorous dinosaurs did not have those formidable teeth for nothing: human sin could not have brought death into the world.

The prominent evangelical naturalist Philip Gosse in his book *Omphalos* (1858) sought to challenge the idea that fossil findings required "geological time".[21] He took up the old question whether Adam and Eve would have had a navel (*omphalos*); and concluded that, being fully human, they would have. If on meeting Adam and seeing his navel, one had asked "How is your mother?", he would have explained that he had not had one, but was created an adult very recently: like John Stuart Mill, but literally, he never was a boy. The navel was misleading. Similarly, the trees in the Garden of Eden were created full grown, and in fruit: had Adam chopped one down, it would (because it was fully a tree) have had rings, from which an observer might have supposed erroneously that it was many years old. Just as humans have navels, and trees have rings, so perhaps the recently-created Earth has fossils that misleadingly imply a past history. The book did not go down well. To agnostics (a term coined by Huxley) it showed the desperate expedients that literal attachment to the Bible entailed; while to believers it showed God unacceptably and incredibly tricking honest searchers after truth.

The Origin of Species

By then Darwin, his barnacle studies finished, had accumulated enough evidence to begin writing a three-volume tome on natural selection; and after being shocked to receive the letter from Alfred Russel Wallace in Malaysia proposing just the same theory, to write the *Origin of Species* as an "abstract", without notes or bibliography, and thus seeming as accessible as *Vestiges*.[22] Ample time was essential if the slow process of natural selection were to produce complex organisms: Darwin took it. An ardent disciple of Lyell, happy to draw blank cheques on the past, he computed that the single episode of denudation of the weald (between the North and South Downs in Kent and Sussex) would have taken three hundred million years. He soon had to revise that downwards a bit in subsequent editions; and then geologists were seriously challenged by William Thomson, the eminent physicist and engineer. Newton had been a knight, Davy a baronet, but Thomson became Lord Kelvin, the first scientist in Britain to be thus honoured. He was involved in the birth of thermodynamics, the science of heat and work: the "absolute" scale of temperature is named after him. People had supposed that the Sun shone on and on because that was its nature: but Thomson, knowing that energy cannot come from nowhere, worked out its age and prospects, assuming it was made of the finest Newcastle coal, and was further fuelled by meteorites and by gravitational collapse. This gave a past and future for the middle-aged luminary of about fifty million years, maybe as much as one hundred million. Then he computed the age of the Earth, assuming it was slowly cooling, radiating heat into space: and this yielded very much the same figure.[23] Scientists delight in such converging calculations, which give powerful reasons for belief. Huxley spoke up for geologists and evolutionists, but could not refute Thomson's formidable quantitative reasoning.

Thomson was a pious man, who began his courses at Glasgow with a prayer: but an Earth fifty or a hundred million years old is very different from one made in 4004BC, and his work did little to comfort literalists. Time's unimaginable abyss was still there. His vision of the end, as the Sun and Earth cooled, led Huxley's disciple H.G.Wells in his *Time Machine* (1895) to imagine evolution going under these conditions "backwards" or "downwards", as humans diverged into two inferior species, and then only invertebrates were left in the endless solar winter as the Sun turned into a cool red giant star.[24] Degeneration became a nightmare vision, fuelling *fin-de-siecle* gloom.[25]

But while Darwinian evolution, or "development" to use the term he preferred, was not automatically progressive, most contemporaries saw it that way. His was a dynamic world of shifting equilibria, very different from clockwork and owing something to both the Romantic movement and the Enlightenment. He could not accept that this long-drawn-out process that had led to us, through the war of nature, famine and death, could be the work of a loving God. He became an agnostic or perhaps a Deist; but he saw evolution as the result of laws acting around us, not chance. And indeed some clergy, including Charles Kingsley, and the parson-naturalist and Fellow of the Geological Society W.S.Symonds in his book *Old Bones,* were immediately happy to recognise him as a discoverer of laws:[26]

> If, after the great discovery of Newton, astronomers and mathematicians had squabbled, and fought, and used hard names and theological arguments as to why the law we find in operation must obtain, and had insisted on reasons for the law, as squared to the chronology and history of the Jews, instead of accepting the knowledge of the law as a law, and working on the basis of that knowledge, astronomy would not have been the science it now is. The force of gravity is a mystery, the history of creation is a mystery, life is a mystery, all God's laws are mysteries. They are laws, nevertheless, and it appears to me that if we let the reasons why and how alone, and studied the effects of the laws more, we should be more likely to arrive at truth....There is a constantly operating, secondary, creational law.... With knowledge of such laws as a basis, we look forward to a magnificent structure, yet to be reared by the investigations of geological, palaeontological, and biological science

But already Huxley was underlining our similarity to the apes, as members of the same natural group; and cartoonists seized upon Darwin's heavy eyebrows to turn him into an ape-man in caricature.[27] In 1863 Lyell published his *Antiquity of Man,* demonstrating with evidence from caves and from archaeological sites that humans had co-existed with animals now extinct, and went back long before 4004BC.[28] Human prehistory was a matter of tens of thousands of years. Lyell, now coming off the fence and becoming in his turn a disciple of Darwin, his protégé, predicted that if we have a common ancestor with the apes the earliest human fossils would be found where they live, in central Africa and in Indonesia. Darwin had included one diplomatic sentence about mankind in the *Origin of Species,* but now it was clear that a literal reading of the first chapters of *Genesis* as science was no longer possible: as Davy had said, revelation does not give us laws of nature. Biblical criticism was at the same time becoming public knowledge in Britain, with the appearance of *Essays and Reviews* in 1860, a few weeks after the *Origin of Species.*[29] The dark backward of time had included our immediate ancestors, and could not be divorced from our story.

Development

Nevertheless, evolution (and so long periods of time) had become the key to explanation of everything by the time Darwin died and was buried in Westminster Abbey in 1882. Just as *Vestiges* came out, John Henry Newman had been pondering his position in the Church of England, and writing the book on the development of doctrine which marked his passage to the Church of Rome.[30] Twenty-five years later Frederick Temple, notorious for his piece in *Essays and Reviews,* became Bishop of Exeter (and subsequently of London, and then Archbishop of Canterbury) and in 1884 delivered the Bampton Lectures at Oxford on the relations of science and religion, where he declared that:[31]:

> To the many partial designs which Paley's Natural Theology points out, and which still remain what they were, the doctrine of Evolution adds the design of a perpetual progress

He noted that whether creation was "a single act done in a moment, or a process lasting through millions of years" was immaterial because the purpose of revelation in the Bible was not to teach science at all, but to teach great spiritual and moral lessons. The Bible took "the facts of nature as they appear to ordinary people". Neither evolution nor geological time need bother the believer: and indeed evolution made us focus very valuably upon creation as an ongoing process rather than the long-past event it was for Deists.

In 1889 *Lux Mundi,* another collection of theological essays by Oxford men, was published under the editorship of the high-churchman and disciple of Pusey, Charles Gore, subsequently a Bishop. By this time evolution was in the air; and J.R.Illingworth wrote one of the essays, on "the Incarnation in Relation to Development", having little difficulty with regard to the compatibility of Biblical doctrine rightly understood with evolutionary ideas and timescale.[32] In 1894 Henry Drummond, delivering the Lowell Lectures in Boston, under the title "the Ascent of Man" (elegantly reversing the title of one of Darwin's books, *The Descent of Man,* 1871) rejoiced in evolution:[33]

Evolution has ushered a new hope into the world. The supreme message of science in this age is that all Nature is on the side of the man who tries to rise. Evolution, development, progress are not only on her programme, these are her programme. For all things are rising, all worlds, all planets, all stars and suns.

This ready acceptance of evolution, for a vast history as well as a vast extent of the universe, and its identification with progress was more characteristic of the time than the gloom of Wells, although it was in fact less Darwinian. For Darwin, in a changing world where niches are to be sought and divergence the rule, creatures might like barnacles evolve from common ancestors with shrimps and crabs, becoming simpler; they might, like crocodiles, stay much the same for aeons; or they might, like primates, become more and more complex in structure and behaviour. He disliked terms like "higher" and "lower", just as natural theologians admiring apt designs would have done: what mattered was adaptation to conditions.

At the end of the century, Arthur Balfour (soon to be Prime Minister) promoted his idea that science just like everything else rested upon belief.[34] Science involved acts of faith, in the uniformity of nature and the reign of natural law; but it had proved its trustworthiness in its sphere, and we should not without good reason doubt its conclusions. Given that our minds are finite, though, we should also not expect that all our knowledge will cohere: there are always going to be things that we do not understand. The revolution in physics in the early twentieth century, when Newtonian mechanics and causality were shaken, seemed to prove him right: and in 1918, facing a complex post-war future, the Council of the Royal Society wanted him to be President, in succession to J.J. Thomson. He found out that the post entailed work, and turned it down, though he became in the 1920s in effect Minister for Science.

Literalism

Not everyone had accepted Buckland's work; there were "scriptural geologists" who insisted that he was playing fast and loose with the Bible, and that the six-days narrative must be taken literally. Similarly, Lyell had his critics, and indeed today geologists accept that there have been some "catastrophes" in the form of mass extinctions in a fairly short time. Darwin met with considerable opposition, from established geologists and biologists as importantly as from clergy; and the Darwinism that became generally adopted in the nineteenth century was more optimistic and bland than his own views. Thomson, the doyen of classical physicists, lived into the years of revolution in physics, when his calculations were overturned by the discovery of radioactivity. If the Sun is a thermonuclear reactor rather than a coal-fired furnace, and the Earth is being warmed by the decay of uranium, then the billions of years of Lyell and Darwin become reasonable again. Also in the early twentieth century, Darwinian evolution by natural selection seemed incompatible with the new science of genetics, which called for gross mutations rather than minute variations as the propellant of development. Balfour was clearly right in pointing to the element of belief in, and the provisional character of, science. Experience shows that well-established pieces of science are in time falsified: can we expect that to happen to geological time?

Darwin set out on *HMS Beagle* as an ordinand and a literal believer in the Bible, and his shipmates sometimes laughed at his naïve beliefs. There were other nineteenth-century men of science who were literalists: Gosse, but more importantly Michael Faraday. But the Bible says nothing about electro-magnetism, and he had no serious difficulties about his various beliefs. The fundamentalism of the twenty-first century is rather different, an aggressive compound of modernity and reaction. When on some creationist website, the claim is made that the Grand Canyon could have been, and indeed was, carved out in a few weeks by the Flood, what are we to say? Balfour had excellent connections in Cambridge and London with the latest science, through distinguished practitioners: he took and recommended the advice of experts. We should surely do the same, although it occasionally happens that the maverick may be the unheard voice crying in the wilderness, as Gregor Mendel perhaps was. The creationists are surely the analogues, in their attitude to science, of those who know that Jesus married Mary Magdalene and settled down to raise a family, because the da Vinci Code says so. Belief-systems in science as in religion have their well-established canons, tried and tested, open to revision as these must be. Expert opinion is a good guide; and false belief will let you down when it comes to practice. We should surely be glad that scientific progress casts light on our other beliefs, and certainly that the idea of creation happening only at one point in the past, an event rather than a process, is a casualty of Lyell and Darwin's science. Of course, living in an open-ended and dynamic world is more alarming and grown-up than inhabiting a clockwork: we have responsibilities, to do with the environment for example, and nobody knows for sure how things will work out. Science is as much about the destruction of old certainties as the building of new ones.

References

1. "The dark backward and abysm of time": W.Shakespeare, *The Tempest,* act 1, scene 2, line 50.
2. A.Fyfe, *Science and Salvation: Evangelical Popular Science Publishing in Victorian Britain* (Chicago: University Press, 2004); D.M.Knight, *Public Understanding of Science: a History of Communicating Scientific Knowledge* (London: Routledge, 2006).
3. A.L.Lavoisier, *Elements of Chemistry* [1790], trans. R.Kerr (New York: Dover, 1965) p. xvii.
4. W.Paley, *Natural Theology* [1802] ed. M.D.Eddy and D.M.Knight (Oxford: University Press, 2006); D.Sobel, *Longitude* (London: Fourth Estate, 2004); J.C.Taylor and A.W.Wolfendale, "John Harrison: Clockmaker and Copley Medallist", *Notes and Records of the Royal Society,* **61** (2007), pp. 53-62.
5. Omar Khayyam, *The Rubáiyát,* trans. E.Fitzgerald (London: Folio Society, 1955) stanza 53.
6. D.Hume, *On Religion* [1779] ed. A.W.Colver and J.V.Price (Oxford: University Press, 1976) p. 241.
7. J.Hutton, *Theory of the Earth,* [1788] ed. V.E.Eyles and G.W.White (Darien, Conn: Hafner, 1970) p. 128.
8. J.Playfair, *Illustrations of the Huttonian Theory of the Earth* [1802] intr. G.W.White (New York: Dover, 1956).
9. J.P.Deleuze, *History and Description of the Royal Museum of Natural History,* (Paris, 1825); M.P.Crosland, *Science Under Control: the French Academy of Sciences, 1795-1914* (Cambridge: University Press, 1992).
10. J.Parkinson, *Organic remains of a Former World* (London: Sherwood, Neely et al., 1804-1811).
11. G.Cuvier, *Essay on the Theory of the Earth,* trans. R.Jameson, 5th edn. (Edinburgh: Blackwood, 1827); *Discours sur les Révolutions du Globe,* ed.Dr. Hoefer (Paris: Firmin-Didot, 1877).
12. H.Torrens, "Mary Anning", in *Oxford Dictionary of National Biography* (Oxford: University Press, 2004).
13. W.Buckland, *Reliquiae Diluvianae,* 2nd edn. (London: John Murray, 1824); D.M.Knight, *Science and Spirituality: the Volatile Connection* (London: Routledge, 2004) pp. 53-73.
14. H.Davy, *Collected Works,* ed. J.Davy (London: Smith, Elder, 1839-40) vol. 7, p.41.
13. C.Lyell, *Principles of Geology* [1830-3], intro. M.J.S. Rudwick (Cramer: Lehre, 1970).
14. W.Buckland, *Geology and Mineralogy, Considered with Reference to Natural Theology,* 2nd ed. (London: Pickering, 1837); M.J.S. Rudwick, *Scenes from Deep Time* (Chicago: UniversityPress, 1992); J.R.Topham, "Beyond the Common Context: the Production and Reading of the Bridgewater Treatises", *Isis* **89** (1998) pp. 233-62.

17. A.Tennyson, *In Memoriam* [1850] ed. S.Shatto and M.Shaw (Oxford: University Press, 1982) sect. 56.
18. J.F.W.Herschel, *Essays from the Edinburgh and Quarterly Reviews, with Addresses and Other Pieces* (London: Longman, 1857) p. 737; *Preliminary Discourse on the Study of Natural Philosophy* [1830] intr. M.Partridge (New York: Johnston, 1966); D.G.King-Hele, ed., *John Herschel, 1792-1871* (London: Royal Society, 1992).
19. J.A.Secord, *Victorian Sensation: the Extraordinary Publication, Reception, and Secret Authorship of "Vestiges of the Natural History of Creation"* (Chicago: University Press, 2000); A.Desmond, J.Moore and J.Browne, *Charles Darwin* (Oxford: University Press, 2007); C.Darwin and A.R.Wallace, *Evolution by Natural Selection,* intr. G. de Beer (Cambridge: University Press, 1958).
20. Tennyson, ref. 17.
21. P.H.Gosse, *Omphalos: an Attempt to Untie the Geological Knot* (London: Van Voorst, 1858): there is a facsimile reprint, intr. by me (London: Routledge and Natural History Museum, 2003); A.Thwaite, *Glimpses of the Wonderful: the Life of Philip Henry Gosse* (London: Faber, 2002).
22. C.Darwin, *On the Origin of Species by Means of Natural Selection, or the Preservation of Favoured Races in the Struggle for Life* (London: John Murray, 1859) pp. 285-7, 489-90: there are facsimile editions in print.
23. W.Thomson (Lord Kelvin), *Popular Lectures and Addresses* (London: Macmillan, 1888-94) vol. 1, pp.356-429, vol. 3, pp. 10-131.
24. H.G.Wells, *The Time Machine* [1895], ed. J.Lawton (London: Dent, 1995).
25. D.Pick, *Faces of Degeneration: a European Disorder, c1848-c1918* (Cambridge:University Press, 1989); M.Hawkins, *Social Darwinism in European and American Thought, 1860-1945: Nature as Model and Nature as Threat* (Cambridge: University Press, 1997).
26. W.S.Symonds, *Old Bones: or Notes for Young Naturalists* (London: Hardwicke, 1860) pp.119-20; N.Cooper ed., *John Ray and his Successors: the Clergymen as Biologist* (Braintree: John Ray Trust, 2000) pp.145-51.
27. T.H.Huxley, *Evidence as to Man's Place in Nature,* [1863], intr. A.Montagu, (Ann Arbor: Michigan University Press, 1959); J.Browne, *Charles Darwin: the Power of Place* (London: Pimlico, 2002).
28. C.Lyell, *The Geological Evidences of the Antiquity of Man, with Remarks on Theories of the Origin of Species by Variation* (London: Murray, 1863).
29. V.Shea and W.Whitla ed., *Essays and Reviews: the 1860 Text and its Reading* (Charlottesville: Virginia UniversityPress, 2000).
30. F.M.Turner, *John Henry Newman: the Challenge to Evangelical Religion* (New Haven: Yale University Press, 2002); S.Gilley, *Newman and his Age* (London: Darton, Longman and Todd, 1990).
31 F.Temple, *The Relations Between Religion and Science* (London: Macmillan, 1885) pp.116-7, 181.
32. J.R.Illingworth in C.Gore ed., *Lux Mundi: a Series of Studies in the Religion of the Incarnation,* 15th ed. (London: Murray, 1899) pp.132-57.
33. H.Drummond, *The Ascent of Man* (London: Hodder, 1894) p. 435.

34. A.J.Balfour, *The Foundations of Belief: being Notes Introductory to the Study of Theology* (London: Longman, 1895).

CHAPTER SIX

SCRIPTURAL GEOLOGISTS AND LIBERAL
ANGLICANS: A RESPONSE TO DAVID KNIGHT

NEIL SPURWAY

Neil Spurway, Emeritus Professor of Exercise Physiology in the University of Glasgow, has Chaired the British Association of Sport and Exercise Sciences, and been President of the Royal Philosophical Society of Glasgow. He has also had a lifelong interest in the Science/Religion interaction. He edited the Centenary series of Glasgow Gifford Lectures ("Nature, Environment and God", Blackwell 1992), now edits the membership journal of the European Society for the Study of Science and Theology, and is the current Chair of the Science and Religion Forum.

Here he takes up Prof Knight's underlying theme of the 19th C confrontation with "deep time", as initially demonstrated by geology and subsequently required by Darwin's account of evolution by natural selection. In counterpoint to Prof Knight's broad overview, Neil Spurway focuses on two groups, one pre- and the other post-Darwinian, both of which have obvious parallels in the current intellectual scene.

Prof Knight's lovely essay is written with the sweep of the life-long historian of ideas. As a scientist, interested in the history of the field, but not a true historian, I would not presume to disagree with any material aspect of his account. Rather, I shall take a more detailed look at some features of the 19th C scene which seem particularly instructive for the present day. My pattern will be:
   1) to say more about a group to whom Prof Knight had space only to allude—the "Scriptural Geologists"—and some of their less extreme contempories
   2) to supplement his comments on the reception of Darwin's *Origin* by contemporary Christian churchmen

3) to point to many similarities but one key difference between the 19th and the 21st C situations.

Scriptural Geology[1]

The Scriptural Geologists, *sensu strictu*, believed that the Genesis account of the creation of the world, and the species which inhabit it, was literally true. In modern parlance, they were "Young Earth Creationists", who held that – whether or not Bishop Usher's calculations were exactly right – the earth was certainly less than 10,000 years old. Alternative conclusions to this were "drawn in the teeth of the authenticated *fact* (sic), 'that in six days the Lord made heaven and earth'!" (James Brown, 1838)[2]. To achieve the stratigraphic record in so short a period, Brown proposed that the laws of physics had been speeded up 100 times or more.

A kindred spirit, George Fairholme[3], inveighed against "the mere laws of nature, as they are called", as being "part of the deceptious evidence of physical facts, seen in a false light". He considered the opinions of "the French school" (Cuvier, Lamarck) "absurd and extraordinary"; most particularly the latter's view that "all the forms of animated beings, as they now exist, must have been gradually developed, as their wants and necessities demanded". Why this is absurd and extraordinary was not explained. Fairholme and Brown are extreme instances of those Scriptural Geologists whom their modern editor, John M Lynch, describes as "classically educated ... dilettantes" ... most of whom had never examined a rock-face in their lives[4].

Such red-necks as these were, however, already a minority. Contrast with them the views, not only of professional geologists such as Lyell, but of the Scottish *theologian* Thomas Chalmers (not to be confused with Robert Chambers, a generation younger, discussed by Prof Knight). As early as 1804, Chalmers wrote:

> There is a prejudice against the speculations of the geologist which I am anxious to remove .... It has been alleged that geology, by referring the origin of the globe to a higher antiquity than is assigned to it by the writings of Moses, undermines our faith in the inspiration of the Bible .... This is a false alarm. The writings of Moses do not fix the antiquity of the globe. [5]

Instead, Chalmers contended that the Genesis account allows for an indefinite gap between the first and third verses of Chap 1. In fact, this "Gap theory". formalised a view to which many were already inclined: Usher's chronology was adhered to only by a minority even in the early

1800's. An alternative picture which was widely hinted at, though less often spelled out, was the "chaos-restitution" model – an extensive but undefined period of chaos after the initial creation (worth comparing with the proposal outlined by Dr Bonting in this volume), which was followed by a re-ordering in six days and then, after a variously calculated further time, a global Deluge.

The broad-minded Chalmers recognised the smallness of "the globe, and 'all that it inherits', in the immensity of creation". But his lament is telling: "… while the most respectful caution, and humility, and steadiness, are seen to preside over every department of moral and physical investigation, theology is the only subject that is suffered to remain the victim of prejudice". *Plus ca change?*

Further into the century, a very different character thought along similar lines. This was a man who had examined countless rock-faces, and was by no means classically educated: Hugh Miller, a stonemason in the remote Scottish county of Cromarty, became so intrigued by observations of the rocks on which he worked that he taught himself geology and "amassed an impressive amount of geological knowledge during … annual field trips"[6]. Towards the end of his life he was frequently invited to lecture in Edinburgh, Glasgow and even London; and he was well versed not only in British but in Continental authors, notably Cuvier and the German biblical scholar Kurtz. Recognizing the "high antiquity" of the rocks, yet initially accepting the Genesis "days" as of 24 hrs, he proposed an immense time-gap between the sixth day of creation and our own times – a similar intellectual recourse to that of Chalmers, except that by day six there was the advantage of a sun to mark out the days! However, in his last and greatest book (1857), Miller came to hold that "the days of creation were not natural, but prophetic days, and stretched far back into the bygone eternity". Thus he re-states what is now designated the "day-age" theory, a proposal with which others, wanting to follow Lyle and Buckland without rejecting scripture, had by then been toying for some time.

Miller's pedagogy is remarkable – steadfastly biblical yet geologically persuasive. He treats the grass and trees of day three (Genesis 1. vv.11-13) as indicating the Carboniferous period, the sea creatures and birds of day five (vv.20-23) as the Oolitic and Cretaceous, and the terrestrial creatures of day six (vv.24-25) as the Tertiary – merging into the human era of vv.26-31. The ongoing seventh day's work is that of moral improvement and redemption. Yet he still sees all the acts of species-creation as separate divine interventions – and claims that each phylum can be seen from the fossil record to have fallen from an original, Divinely-fashioned perfection. In no-one is the tension between conflicting determinations – to believe scripture literally yet follow the evidence of one's eyes to its most economical conclusion – more evident.

A contemporary of Miller's, but at the opposite extreme in terms of formal training and academic status, was John Pye Smith, FRS, DD[7]. As liberal-minded as Chalmers had been, Smith rejected all versions of the six-day creation claim. Not only are there "physical evidences of the most decisive kind, that each of those successive conditions was of extremely long duration", but the formation of carboniferous limestone required an atmospheric level of carbon dioxide which would have been fatal to air-breathing organisms as we know them. This is a very early recognition of atmospheric change.

Smith emphasises the adaptedness of organisms to particular environments, and the essentiality of changes in them when conditions alter. Accordingly, he notes the impossibility of their all surviving simultaneously in either Eden or the ark. Consistently with this, he insists again and again that God rules his universe according to a harmonious plan: "a system which has no shocks, no breaks, no failures, to need the interposition of correcting and repairing". He "humbly thinks that, for the honour of God and the interests of genuine religion, it is our duty to protest against the practice of bringing in miraculous interpositions, to help out the exigiencies of arbitrary and fanciful theories. No: our 'God is the Rock,' eternal and unchangeable in his attributes …". One must thoroughly pursue a science before one can validly judge it. When striving to summarise for an outsider, who has not subjected himself to this discipline, "the multitude and diversity tend to embarrass us, and the difficulty lies chiefly in selection and arrangement". By contrast, the unscientific dogmatists such as Browne and Fairholme, "occupied by studies only in the closet", "speak and write with a confidence in the direct proportion of their incompetency".

Smith also quotes Cuvier: "May not Natural History one day have her Newton?". The ground is prepared, but the great insight is still awaited. 16 years Smith's book – and just two years after Miller's last and best – Charles Darwin will publish *The Origin of Species*, and humanity's view of its world will be changed forever.

Reactions to Darwin

The Origin of Species (1859) irresistibly documented the course of evolution *and,* within the limits of the biology of the day, proposed the mechanism of it – Natural Selection, from a vast diversity of spontaneous variations. Such an account need not be interpreted as a denial of the hand of God, only denial that it was an endlessly fussy hand. Darwin himself suggested that he was showing, not *that* God was not at work, but how He was at work. (Darwin's exact position is uncertain, as Prof Knight implies, but my own sense is that, in 1859 Darwin himself thought this way, though his sense of Divine involvement was to diminish in later years.) Adam Sedgwick, Professor of Geology at Cambridge and Darwin's one-time mentor, abhorred his pupil's conclusions, and responded in terms which would have won the approval of the Scriptural Geologists – that the 'transmutation of species' was 'a theory no better than a phrensied dream'. Yet Charles Kingsley, polymathic author and naturalist cleric, thanked Darwin for a copy of *The Origin* in these terms[8]:

> I have gradually learned to see that it is just as noble a conception of Deity, to believe that He created primal forms capable of self-development into all forms needful *pro tempore* and *pro loco*, as to believe that He required a fresh act of intervention to supply the lacunas which he himself had made. I question whether the former be not the loftier thought.

And again, more strongly:

> Now that they have got rid of an interfering God, a master-magician as I call it – they have to choose between the absolute empire of accident and a living immanent, ever-working God.

Many of us at the present day would consider that these words of Kingsley's embody what is still the essential religious response to Darwin and, *mutatis mutandis*, to other scientific revolutionaries. And who has bettered the phrasing? If Jaques Monod or Richard Dawkins had thought of "the absolute empire of accident" they would surely have rubbed their hands in glee!

Somewhat later, however, a stream of thought grew up which was happy to conceive evolution as the working out of Divine ideas through time, but for which the concept that variations occurred randomly and their subsequent survival or extinction depended upon competitive struggle – "Nature, red in tooth and claw" – seemed unacceptably at odds with the picture of an all-wise, all-loving and all-powerful God. Henry Drummond, to whom Prof Knight refers, was one of these. His version of Darwinism had altruistic cooperation, a struggle not for the individual's survival but for that of others, built into the account. The problem of 'natural evil' is of comparable concern to modern writers such as Holmes Ralston III and Christopher Southgate[9], but they cannot accept Drummond's solution.

My final Victorian figure is the high church Oxford theologian, Aubrey Moore, who held that:

> The scientific evidence in favour of evolution, *as a theory* is infinitely more Christian than the theory of "special creation". For it implies the immanence of God in nature, and the omnipresence of His creative power. Those who oppose the doctrine of evolution in defence of a "continued intervention" of God, seem to have failed to notice that a theory of occasional intervention implies as its correlative *a theory of ordinary absence*.[10]

That's it! That's where we have to be. Deism cannot suffice: our understanding of God's relation to the created world must be one of immanence. In essence, all the world-class theologians of evolution writing in the last 30 years have thought this way – and Arthur Peacocke, the *doyen* of this field in Britain, actually used a phrase of Moore's as the title of his late collection of essays on the subject.[11]

If, to complete this look back to Victorian thinking on biology in relation to theology, we return to my first section, we unmistakably see there, too, the complete gamut of possible stances *vis-à-vis* Creationism. The current generation of Young Earth Creationists sound exactly like Brown and Fairholme. "Gap" thinking may no longer be common, but "day-age" theories such as Miller's are by no means dead. Yet the liberality of mind shown by Chalmers in 1804 could not be better expressed today; and Smith's frustrations, at the difficulty of imparting any sense of the true force of a discipline such as palaeontology to the uninitiated, and at confidence based on superficial knowledge, are feelings we can echo precisely despite the passage of 170 years.

Other aspects of the modern situation

The common theme, running through both Prof Knight's essay and my own, has been the 19th C encounter with deep time. It was the first, and arguably the greatest, challenge of science to faith in the modern era; yet it was a challenge, as we have both sought to show, which to people of vision embodied no threat, only an immense opportunity. It may be that part of the difficulty found by proponents of the so-called "Intelligent Design", the modern a-theological variant of Creationism, in understanding the power of evolutionary development is that they still lack sufficient intuitive sense of how long evolution has been operating. That apart, however, deep geological time is no longer as massive a consideration as it was in the 19th C.

Now we have cosmology instead. Since Einstein, Hubble and Lemaître, the even deeper time for which the Universe itself has existed has become the greater challenge to the imagination. Augustine's perception, that time itself began with the creation of the Universe, seems more and more vindicated. We want to ask what was "before" Creation, what is "outside" space ... we want to, but we cannot, for the words in quote-marks have no meaning. Understanding existence was hard for the Victorians, but I'm not sure it isn't harder still for us.

However, in this book the implications of cosmology are the themes of other essays.

References

1. All quotations under this subheading can be found in the facsimile republication of books by eight pre-Darwinian writers, *Creationism and Scriptural Geology, 1814-1857*, ed John M Lynch (Bristol: Thoemmes Press, 7 vols, 2002).
2. James Brown, *Reflections on Geology Suggested by the Perusal of Dr Buckland's Bridgewater Treatise* (1838). Reprinted in ref 1, vol. 1.
3. George Fairholme, *A General View of the Geology of Scripture* (1833). Reprinted as vol. 4 of ref 1.
4. Lynch, *Introduction* to ref. 1, vol. 1.
5. Thomas Chalmers: an essay of 1804, cited in ref.1, vol. 1.
6. Hugh Miller, *The Testimony of the Rocks; Or, Geology in its Bearing on the Two Theologies, Natural and Revealed* (1857). Reprinted as vol. 7 of ref 1.
7. John Pye Smith, *On the Relation Between the Holy Scriptures and Some Parts of Geological Science* (1843). Reprinted as vol. 6 of ref. 1.
8. Francis Darwin, ed., *The Life and Letters of Charles Darwin* (London: John Murray, 1887) vol 2. For further discussion of all matters under this subheading, see also *Darwinism and Divinity*, ed. John Durant (Oxford: Blackwell, 1985).
9. Holmes Rolston III, *Genes, Genesis and God: Values and their Origins in Natural and Human History* (Cambridge: University Press, 1999); John F Haught, *God after Darwin: A Theology of Evolution* (Boulder, CO: Westview Press, 2000); Christopher Southgate, 'God and Evolutionary Evil: Theodicy in the Light of Darwinism', *Zygon* **37** (2002) p 803; *The Good and the Groaning: Evolution, suffering and the call of humanity* (Louisville, KE: Westminster John Knox Press, due June 2008).
10. Aubrey Moore, *Science and Faith* (London: Kegan, Paul, Trench, Trubner, 1889).
11. Arthur Peacocke, *Evolution: The Disguised Friend of Faith?* (Philadelphia, PA: Templeton Foundation Press, 2004).

Chapter Seven

Creation and the Abrahamic Faiths

Keith Ward

Keith Ward, FBA, has a B. Litt. in Philosophy from Oxford, and a DD from Cambridge. He is currently Professor of Divinity of Gresham College, London, having retired from the Regius Chair of Divinity at Oxford; before that he held a Chair at King's College, London. His many books include "God, Chance and Necessity" (Oneworld, 1996), "Pascals' Fire" (Oneworld, 2006), and "The Big Questions in Science and Religion (Forthcoming, Templeton Press, 2008)".

In this paper, based on his plenary lecture at the 2006 conference, Prof Ward contrasts two viewpoints on the relation of God to creation, each of which has been espoused, at different times, by leading theologians in all three Abrahamic faiths – the classical view, of a changeless and impassible God, and the recent one, of a God involved with and affected by the created world.

Interpreting Creation

A reasonable, if partial, definition of God is that God is the supremely perfect creator of everything other than God. God is perfect in the sense that God is, as Anselm put it, 'that than which nothing more valuable can be conceived'.[1] God is creator, as being the cause of all finite things through an act of conscious intention.

The belief that God is the creator of the cosmos is shared between all the Abrahamic faiths, and provides an underlying unity between them. Yet there are many different ways in which creation can be interpreted. I shall mention two major interpretations that can be found in Judaism, Christianity, and Islam, and show how they each reflect the best scientific and philosophical thought of a specific historical epoch. I do not thereby mean to imply that the interpretations are limited to that historical epoch. But it is true that they arose at a time that was particularly conducive to the formulation of one key interpretation.

It is perfectly possible to be a devout Abrahamic believer and not have any interpretation of the doctrine of creation. It is enough to say that the cosmos is created by a perfect spiritual being, from whom all things issue and to whom all things return. Yet the doctrine of creation has come under philosophical attack, especially since the eighteenth century in Europe. And some understandings of the doctrine are unacceptably anthropomorphic. So it is important that there should be a philosophical interpretation of the doctrine of creation that is able to counter the attacks of atheists, to refine the cruder versions of religious literalism, and so to present the doctrine as what it is, a philosophically profound and plausible account of the nature of reality.

The two main interpretations I shall consider are that of Thomas Aquinas, in the thirteenth century, which is based on the thought of Aristotle, and a twentieth century view that owes much to the Idealist philosophy of Hegel and the Process philosophy of Whitehead. There are other interpretations in existence, and perhaps more yet to come. It would be wrong to think these were the only possible views, or that one of them was so obviously correct that no other was necessary.

The Thomist view, however, has a good claim to be called the "classical" view. It was shared between Judaism (in Maimonides, for example), Islam (in Al Gazzali), and Aquinas, and is still the basis of major schools of thought in those faiths. The more recent view is also found in Judaism (in Abraham Heschel), in Islam (in Mohammed Iqbal), and in Christianity (Karl Barth). I shall call it, for convenience, the "relational" view.

The Thomist view

Before the sixteenth century it was widely agreed within all the Abrahamic traditions that the Greeks, especially Plato and Aristotle, had perfected the forms of philosophical thought. If one wanted a sophisticated intellectual defence of religious doctrines, it was therefore to the Greek philosophers that one turned. The doctrine of creation itself did not originate with the ancient Greeks. They did not formulate such a doctrine, and they never forged a union between philosophy and the religious beliefs of the Greek city-states. But they provided the concepts in terms of which the prophetic doctrine of creation (probably developed differences of value (of desirability) between such states. Some states are of greater intrinsic value than others – for instance, rich and complex states of beauty are of greater value to a conscious being than simple expanses of monochrome paint. We do not have to rank all possible states in an exact order. But we may assume that an all-knowing being that was not subject to decay and death, and was not in a competitive situation with other similar beings, would be able to rank many possible states with dispassionate objectivity.

God could then, being all-powerful, make actual some or all of the more desirable possible states, and take pleasure in contemplating them. We would then have a broadly Aristotelian God, finding fulfilment and happiness in the contemplation of its own nature. But that nature would include the conception, evaluation, actualisation and contemplation of many possible states out of the total array of possible states in the all-knowing divine mind. That seems to be a coherent concept of a supremely perfect being.

God's consciousness

Some philosophers would object that the properties of conceiving, evaluating, actualising, and contemplating are mental properties. And mental properties can only exist where there are very complex physical entities like brains. Mental states are, or at least are causally dependent upon, brain states. So this hypothesis of a totally unembodied mind is still incoherent.

I think that theists are perfectly entitled to reply that the hypothesis of the causal dependence of mental states upon brain states is just that – a hypothesis. It is not at all a necessary truth, or even a well-established theory. Of course human mental states are causally dependent upon human brain states. No one disputes that – though there is much dispute about whether mental states are reducible to brain states, and about whether mental states have causal influence on their neural substrates.

But if you ask whether it is conceivable that there could be a knowing, evaluating, causally efficacious, and appreciating consciousness, without any physical embodiment, it seems to me that the answer must be 'yes'. It is nothing more than a limitation of imagination to deny the very possibility of such a being. And theism rests on the affirmation that such a consciousness is in fact the most obvious and most primary form of existent.

When we ask about a perfect being, it seems obvious that such a being must be conscious. It must have a rich and beautiful experience, capable between the eighth to sixth centuries BCE) could be philosophically developed.

The "Good"

The first thing Plato and Aristotle did was to frame a notion of divine perfection. Plato spoke of "the Good", the supreme Form in which all things participate, a union of the good and beautiful.[2] Aristotle spoke of God as *noesis noeseos*, a supreme understanding that was supremely happy in the contemplation of its own perfection.[3]

They were asking what possible being or state would constitute supreme perfection. For many modern philosophers there is no such thing. There are lots of different good things, and not everyone agrees on what is good anyway. So all we have are lists of largely incompatible objects of desire. In the absence of desiring agents, there are no "goods", and there is no one state that could unite all possible goods in one perfect reality. Subjectivity and diversity are the key words for many modern philosophers. There are many different desirable states, all of them subjective, and not all of them are obtainable at the same time or by the same being. So the very idea of a perfect being is incoherent.

In response to such objections, that were well known to medieval thinkers, what had to be defended was the objectivity and the unity of goods, of worth-while states. The general form of defence was to describe a set of states that could be universally agreed by all rational agents to be desirable for their own sake. These would be "intrinsic goods", states that it would be reasonable for every desiring agent to want.

Among such goods we would count knowledge, for it is always reasonable to want to know something rather than be ignorant of it. If it is objected that we might prefer not to know such bad things as the time of our own death, or how we are going to die, then we would add power, so that we can avoid death or suffering if we wish. And we would add happiness, since it is always preferable to be happy than to be sad. So a being that had maximal knowledge, together with maximal power and maximal happiness, would be objectively good. All rational agents would agree that such a being was intrinsically good. And if its goodness was maximal – greater than that of any other possible being – it would indeed be supremely good.

These are, it turns out, the major properties of God. Maximal knowledge, power, and happiness (beatitude) are the main attributes of God. There is no apparent reason why such a being could not exist; it is a coherent concept. God would know all possible states. There are of conveying a sense of totally satisfying value. One of the nearest analogies we can think of for it is the contemplation of a great work of art or music. Such an experience is worth-while for its own sake, and is the natural fulfilment of consciousness, which always wills the good as the present object of awareness.

Consciousness by nature tends to awareness of the good. Goodness by nature calls for its actual contemplation, and thus its realisation, by consciousness. So consciousness and goodness are integrally intertwined. Plato's Form of the Good is also the Supreme Consciousness. Theism postulates that such a consciousness is capable of full existence without any physical embodiment. It goes further, and asserts that nothing physical would exist unless it was brought into existence by that consciousness.

For the physical cosmos is one actualisation of a set of possible states that exist in the mind of God. The actualisation, we may reasonably suppose, takes place because of an evaluation of those possible states by God. They are actualised for the sake of their value or goodness. It is in this sense that the created universe is said by the Abrahamic faiths to be good. It is actualised for the sake of the distinctive and otherwise unobtainable sorts of value that it realises.

It is now possible to see the connection between the perfection of God and creation. Theists have always hesitated to say that God has to create a universe. That is because, if God has maximal power, then God presumably has maximal freedom to exercise that power or not. And the possession of such freedom seems incompatible with saying that God is compelled to create some universe.

This is a difficult issue to decide. All would agree that God is not "compelled" to create. But compulsion is being forced against one's will by another. There is no other being that has the power to compel God to do anything. Yet some things belong to God's nature by necessity. For instance, as the supremely perfect being, God is necessarily maximally knowing and powerful. God is not compelled to be maximally knowing. Yet God has no choice in the matter. It is God's essential nature to be maximally knowing. That is not a restriction on the divine being. It is part of the divine perfection.

In a similar way, it could be part of the divine perfection to be creative. Goodness, as Aquinas says, naturally tends to diffuse itself, to share itself with others.[4] We cannot say that there is any sort of duty on God to share the divine goodness with others. But the divine goodness – which is the contemplation of beauty – may by nature desire that such contemplation should be shared by other conscious beings. After all, if it is good that one being should contemplate beauty, it is also good that many beings should do so, and should do so in different ways.

Only one being can contemplate goodness as God does, because God is the source of all possibility, and there cannot be more than one such source. But there could be other conscious beings that could share in the contemplation of some of the possibilities that exist in God, in their own finite manner. That would add to the sorts of actualised, contemplated, goodness that exist, and to the number of beings that contemplate them.

Without implying that God has a duty to create such beings, it would certainly be good for God to do so. So if God is good by nature, then it might be natural for God to create finite conscious beings, not by any sort of compulsion, but by a natural expression of the divine nature.

It is because of this that creation can be spoken of as causality through an intentional act. God contemplates all possibilities, evaluates them, and freely chooses to actualise some of them in a universe that will generate finite conscious agents. The reason for speaking of an intentional act is that God is conscious of all possibles, and selects some of them for a good and consciously entertained reason. This act is entirely compatible with the nature of God. It is not compelled, and it is not arbitrary and irrational. It is a conscious and creative decision, that brings new goods into existence, but that does not change the nature of God as the one and only supremely perfect source of all beings.

Imperfect matter

If creation is a natural expression of the perfection of God, why did Plato and Aristotle not think of it? It seems to me that the fundamental reason was that they thought that matter was basically chaotic or imperfect. In Plato's *Timaeus*, the Demiurge or world architect shapes matter in accordance with the eternal Forms as well as possible.[5] But the Forms can never be perfectly embodied in matter. Human souls need to escape from embodiment, from bodies that are the tombs of the soul, to a freer and wholly spiritual life.

Aristotle did not agree with that, but he did agree that matter is intrinsically 'unformed', and that it carries with it the permanent possibility of decay and dissolution. Any perfect being, he thought, must be beyond decay, and therefore beyond the transience of time, untouched by the imperfections of the sublunary realm. A supremely perfect being will exist beyond change and time, and can have no real relation to a material world of change and time. So matter imitates perfection from afar, but never truly shares in it. God contemplates the divine perfection, untouched by and, it seems, unaware of, the sufferings of the physical cosmos. Indeed, it would impair the perfection of the divine experience if it was aware of suffering. So in order to be perfect, God must not participate in the imperfect material world in any real way.

There is a paradox here, that the perfect being should be all-knowing, but is precluded from knowing anything imperfect – and that is, in our universe, almost everything. The Greek view avoids the problem of evil by supposing that God did not create matter, and so is not responsible for it. But this produces another paradox, that the perfect being should be all-powerful, but is precluded from having perfect power over matter, which is almost everything we humans know.

When medieval thinkers tried to resolve these paradoxes, they naturally tried to preserve the omniscience and omnipotence of God. If anything, they inflated the meaning of maximal knowledge and power, which had originally been very vaguely defined, so that God knew and could do or prevent anything that could be stated without self-contradiction – including the past, the future, and the existence of all the evil and suffering in creation. It is not clear that maximal knowledge and power entail such an interpretation. There might, for all we know, be necessary limits on the power even of a maximally powerful being, limits that follow from the nature of that being itself.

Impassibility and changelessness

Aquinas accepted the "capacity to know and do anything that can be stated without self-contradiction" interpretation of divine knowledge and power. Yet he also agreed with the Greek view that God was impassible, incapable of suffering, and therefore of having any truly empathetic knowledge of what suffering is like. He held, as a Christian, that God suffered when Jesus died on the cross. But he construed this as saying that the human nature of Jesus suffered, but the divine nature did not, because it could not, suffer. It is only correct to say that God suffered because Jesus has both a human and a divine nature. The divine nature remains impassible, and so God's beatitude is not affected by the human suffering.

It follows that divine knowledge, for Aquinas, is knowledge of all things insofar as they exist in the divine being. It is not a responsive knowledge of the world, obtained by apprehending the world. It is a knowledge of the ideas of things which, as Anselm put it, are more real in the divine mind than the empirical instantiations of those ideas.

God, being the creator of space and time, and being changeless in perfection, is also timeless. So God's power must be such that it is compatible with lack of change in the divine being. That again means that God cannot be responsive to things that happen in the universe, as though divine power was just a reaction to things that happen outside God. Rather, divine power is wholly creative. It timelessly brings into being everything that is, in every time and place. It does so, being timeless and therefore without the distinction between before and after, in one and the same creative act. It follows that creation is not an act that occurs *before* the genesis of the universe. Creation, for Aquinas and the classical tradition, is the non-temporal dependence of every time and space upon a timeless and spaceless reality that has the nature, analogically speaking, of consciousness and will.

It follows that divine power is the complete timeless determination of all things, including the free acts of creatures, the prayers they utter and the responses to those prayers. It is not possible for God to leave any creature undetermined in its being, since all things are determined by the divine power. Nor is it possible for God to do new and unforeseen things, since that would entail change in the divine being, which is impossible.

I believe this classical view of divine knowledge and power to be coherent. But for many nineteenth and twentieth century thinkers, it seems not after all to represent maximal knowledge and power. For it excludes all specific knowledge of suffering creatures – at least, the sort of knowledge that consists in knowing what it feels like to suffer. And it excludes the possibility of God doing anything new, or reacting in an original way to the free acts of creatures.

For classical theists, "knowing what suffering feels like" is not part of divine knowledge, and is not a perfection at all. And the ability to do quite new and original things is not a perfection either, for God's perfection is immutable, and contains no mere potentiality. God, for Aquinas, is purely actual, without any unrealised potentiality, and it is in that sense that God is not only all-powerful, but actually realises all the possibilities of the divine nature fully.

It requires a change of mind-set to see participative knowledge of suffering, and creative and responsive action, as intrinsic goods. Classical theists cannot see the point of allowing any sort of suffering in God, or of permitting God to respond to the acts of finite beings, rather than seeing God as the one wholly originative author of all actions and events.

That change of mind-set occurred in the sixteenth century with a change from the Greek assertion of the superiority of conceptual thought to empirical observation, and the superiority of the timeless and universal over the temporal and particular. The authority of Aristotle was overthrown by the rise of the "new science", based on experiment and observation, and the mathematical description of the behaviour of physical entities.

A God in relation to Creation

Henceforth, what was "real" were not universal ideas or essences, of which finite particulars were only the imperfect expressions. Rather, reality consisted of constantly changing particulars, and universal ideas were seen as abstractions from the continual flux of reality. The rise of science saw a revolution in ways of seeing reality. At its extreme, this led to the philosophy of materialism, for which only physical particulars are real, and consciousness itself becomes some sort of by-product or illusion. But in a less extreme form, it was seen that empirical observation is an ultimate test of theoretical truth, and that particular events have their own proper reality, and are not just partial exemplifications of universal truths.

If one is influenced by this change of view, then any form of complete knowledge must include knowledge of particulars in all their uniqueness and in their full character. If this involves participative knowledge of suffering – knowing what it is like to suffer – then the idea of divine beatitude must be interpreted so as to include such knowledge. For this reason, the twentieth century Jewish writer Abraham Heschel described God as a "passionate God", involved in the joys and sorrows of creatures.[6]

This is a deeply relational concept of God, and it sees part of divine perfection as lying in relationship to creatures, and as involving something like risk and frustration even for God. But Heschel is clear that the maximal power of God is not thereby compromised. God chooses to suffer such risk and frustration, and there is no possibility of final defeat for God. The life of God will include something like suffering, but it will be suffering that is transformed by an infinitely greater joy – which entails that all finite suffering will come to an end, and be either transformed or eliminated.

For such a relational view, God chooses not to determine every creaturely act, but leaves a degree of freedom to rational creatures. This is a limitation of divine power, but it is a voluntary limitation, and once again the divine power is such that all creaturely freedom will eventually be brought under the good purposes of God, either by transformation or elimination.

The good that is attained by a relational view of divine creation is obtained at the price of some analogy of suffering and of limitation of power in God. But the good is that of a real relationship of shared experience and of co-operation, a relationship ultimately of love. Such a relationship may indeed be considered a great enough value to permit a reconception of the nature of divine beatitude and power.

The views compared

It is not my purpose to adjudicate between the classical and the relational concepts of creation. I mainly wish to illustrate that there are different ways of conceiving the divine perfections, and the nature of creation, that are consistent with a basic belief in creation.

The classical view insists that "maximal knowledge" must include knowledge of the future, and that "maximal power" must include the power to do anything that is logically possible (that is stateable in a non-contradictory sentence). However, the classical view also entails that there is at least one sort of knowledge God cannot have – knowledge of what it is like to feel suffering. And there is at least one sort of power that God cannot have – the power to do something new and unforeseen, or to respond to free acts of creatures.

Relational views sieze upon these difficulties, and propose that they can be largely resolved if divine perfection is taken to include some form of temporality, change, and relationship. Perhaps the Greeks were wrong to think that a perfect being has to be wholly changeless. The standard Greek argument for this is that all change is either for better or for worse. But God cannot either improve or deteriorate, and so change seems to be ruled out for God.

One can simply deny the axiom that all change is for better or worse. God may always be perfect, in always having the maximal knowledge at any time, and yet may apprehend different goods at different times, without it being possible to rank these apprehensions on a common scale of better and worse.

It can be said that it might actually be better for a being successively to apprehend many different sorts of goods, rather than to be unable to apprehend true succession (since for a perfect being on the classical view all things are supposed to be apprehended 'at the same time', or in one act).

Time and Potentiality

If time is real, then knowledge of things in time may have to be temporal. That would entail change in the apprehender as well as in the object apprehended. Thus one might argue, as the philosopher Richard Swinburne does,[7] that any maximally knowing being would have to know time as it truly is – temporally and successively. The past, being completed and unchangeable, would be wholly known. The present would be a constantly changing reality. It could be wholly known, but as something in process of change, not as changeless. The future would not exist, and so could not be known as if it existed.

That does not mean that God would know nothing about the future. To the extent that God controls the future, and has already decided what it will be, God will know the future perfectly. But God might decide not to control the future completely – for example, allowing finite agents to have some, though not total, causal power over it. Or God might not have decided exactly what the future will be, leaving the possibility of new creative action for God as well as for creatures.

It might even be held that the nature of Scriptural prophecy reflects such a situation rather well. The prophecies are very often rather general in nature, and the details of what actually happens are often slightly different from the predictions. Thus, in the Christian case, even if a Messiah is predicted, and even if Christians think the prediction is fulfilled, no-one can reasonably argue that Jesus of Nazareth is exactly what was predicted. One way of accounting for this is to say that God decided to ensure that a Messiah would exist, but was free to respond to historical events by adjusting the details to new circumstances. A similar thing could be said about Prophet Mohammad or about the Jewish prophecies of exile and return.

All this means that God will not be a "purely actual" being, without any potentiality for new actions. On the contrary, God will contain infinite potentialities – and that is a perfectly coherent interpretation of the phrase "all-powerful" – containing all possibilities.

It may be that the possible states are interconnected in subtle ways that it is impossible for human minds to discern. They may be interconnected in such a way that some states entail others at a deep level, and that the human capacity to formulate coherent sentences about individual states fails to capture such interconnections. In other words, there are entailments between states that humans fail to discern, because humans cannot see the necessary connections that obtain in the real world.

This means that there will be real connections of necessity in reality that may not be captured by specific sentences in a human language. Some logicians may deny this possibility. But if we take due account of the frailty of the human mind, it will not seem strange that human languages may not be able to reflect the true nature of reality with perfect accuracy. Only if we could know the mind of God, and the ultimate structure of the cosmos, could we confidently claim that anything we can state in a consistent sentence is a real possibility in the world. It may well be doubted that the human mind is quite as perceptive. It is amazing that we can grasp the intelligible structure of reality to a great degree. It would not be surprising if our grasp was not total and perfect. In that case, we will not be able to say that just because we can describe a state without contradiction, it must be possible for God to bring that state about.

To take an over-simplified example, I may be able to imagine everyone who jumps off a cliff being gently wafted to earth without harm. Then I may complain that God should not allow people to fall to their deaths, when it is quite possible for God to save them all. But the truth probably is that I simply cannot see the consequences of breaking the laws of gravity to order in this way. The whole structure of the cosmos would have to be very different if laws could be broken whenever they threatened to cause harm to sentient beings. In order to discover whether or not this is so, we would have to be able to trace out all the consequences of having a cosmos like that, as opposed to one in which we actually live. It might well be argued that humans are not able to do this competently.

So there might be good reasons for leaving the laws of nature intact, even if that entails the suffering of sentient beings. Because of the nature of the creation, God will not be able to do many things which we seem to be able to imagine and even describe. So, for example, if God decides that it is good to leave some creatures free to decide their own futures within limits, then God cannot also determine (and thus know) exactly what they will do.

For a relational view of divine perfection, then, maximal knowledge and power may involve limits, that would be unacceptable for a classical view, on knowing the future and on determining all events in the universe. I do not think logic alone will resolve this dispute. Much will depend on what one thinks "perfection" is, and there is no consensus on that.

The fact that there is dispute does not mean that there is incoherence. What is important is to see that these are deeply rational disputes, that bring human reason to the edge of its competence. It is clearly more difficult to establish coherence or incoherence that we may at first have thought. But the doctrine of creation as such, whether classical or relational, remains a highly plausible account of the ultimate nature of reality.

Necessary God, necessary Creation?

I will end by pointing out that the scientific search for a "Theory of Everything", an absolute explanation for the existence of the universe, which would not stand in need of any further explanation, is closely paralleled by these philosophical explorations of the idea of divine creation.

The postulate of God is that there is a logical space in which all possible states of affairs exist. This space is necessary and immutable, since possibilities are eternally what they are, and there is no alternative to the exhaustive set of all possible states. For a theist, this logical space is the mind of God. The answer to the misformed question, 'Who made God?' is that God is not the sort of being that can come into being or pass away. God, the actual reality in which all possibities exist, is necessarily existent, if anything is possible at all. So the answer to the question, 'Why is God the way God is?' is that God is, uniquely, necessarily what God is.

When cosmologists search or wish for a Theory of Everything, they are seeking something that would have the necessity belonging to mathematical truths, combined with some principle that would cause those truths to generate an actual physical universe. Steven Weinberg once supposed that there might be a "final theory" in the sense that there might be just one "logically isolated theory, with no undetermined constants, that is consistent with the existence of intelligent beings".[8]

Such a mathematical entity would have to select just one possible universe if intelligent beings were to exist. But three major things remain puzzling about that final mathematical theorem. One is the sense in which a mathematical theorem can actually exist without any mental or physical embodiment. Another is why the existence of intelligent beings should be important to it. And the third is what could enable pure mathematics to actually produce a physical reality – what, as Stephen Hawking put it, could put 'the fire in the equations'.

A possible answer to all these questions is offered by Martin Rees, the Astronomer Royal, in terms of a multiverse.[9] If all possible universes exist, perhaps fluctuating into existence out of a quantum vacuum, then intelligent beings will exist in one of them, and (if Weinberg's supposition is correct) that will be this one.

But the problem still exists of what sort of law it is, presumably logically antecedent to all possible universes, which causes a multiverse to exist. And there is the additional problem of ontological promiscuity – is it really more economical or elegant or plausible to think all possible universes exist than to think there is a necessary being, God, which conceives all possible universes but only actually creates some (and maybe only one) of them?

I do not think a theist should ridicule these ideas, or pretend to have a better scientific hypothesis. But the theist may suggest, with due deference, that a necessarily existing God, the ground of all possibilities, does not seem an odder supposition than a self-existent set of extremely complicated quantum laws. To place all mathematical theorems in a cosmic mind seems a good home for them. And to see the existence of finite intelligent beings as desirable, and therefore selectable for the sake of their possible goodness, seems an eminently reasonable, if non-scientific, form of explanation.

This actual universe, and any other actual universe there is, comes into being, according to the doctrine of creation, for the sake of the distinctive values it actualises. There is thus a reason for the existence of the universe that is rooted in the very nature of things.

Obviously such an absolute explanation for the existence of the universe is not comprehensible by any finite mind. It is an explanation nonetheless, for it affirms that there is a reason for things being as they are, and that reason is rooted in a combination of necessity and value. To say that the universe is ultimately intelligible is not to say that we now understand it fully. But it is to say that it can be understood, which is an important corner-stone of science.

The doctrine of creation, it is important to remember, is not primarily a scientific hypothesis. It arises from a philosophical exploration of a revealed prophetic truth. There is more than one way of interpreting it, and the two main ways I have mentioned depend closely upon the best scientific understandings of the universe that were available when they were formulated, and upon personal evaluations of what perfection is.

We cannot call the creation hypothesis a scientific one, because there is no mathematical description of creation as a physical process that could be used to predict the formation of future universes. Creation is an intentional act by a non-physical ultimate reality, and natural science does not deal in such matters. But the doctrine of creation shares with science a quest for the fullest possible understanding of our universe and the reasons for its nature and existence. And a theist may be bold enough to suggest that the absolute explanation of the universe may lie beyond science – though it will have to be consilient with science. It may lie in a form of ultimate axiological or personal explanation. Having accepted appeal to ultimate mathematical necessities, it will add a reference to values for the sake of which the genesis of a universe might be rationally explained. And that is the fire that will turn possibilities into actualities.

Belief in creation is as far from being "blind faith" as it is possible to get. It is faith, but faith in the ultimate intelligibility of being. It shares with science a determination to understand the universe as fully as possible, and a faith that such understanding is possible. For the

Abrahamic religions, however, the absolute explanation of the universe lies beyond scientific description, in the nature and will of God, whose glory is seen in the splendour of creation, and personal knowledge of whom is given in the disclosures of the divine being given through the prophets. In that way, Abrahamic faith unites understanding and love, necessity and freedom, truth and beauty, in a way that is enriching and illuminating for human life, that motivates both the pursuit of scientific understanding, and a moral commitment to realising in the fullest way those values for the sake of which the universe was created .

References

1. Anselm, *Proslogion*, chs 1 and 2.
2. Plato, *The Republic*, 514-520*.
3. Aristotle, *Metaphysics*, 12, 6-9*.
4. Thomas Aquinas, *Summa Theologiae,* 1a. 19. 2: "A thing has a natural tendency .. .to spread its own good to others".
5. Plato, *Timaeus*, 48*.
6. Abraham Heschel, *The Prophets* (New York: Harper, 1962) p. 224: "God is moved and affected by what happens in the world, and reacts accordingly".
7. Richard Swinburne, *The Coherence of Theism* (Oxford: Clarendon Press, 1977) ch. 12.
8. Steven Weinberg, *Dreams of a Final Theory* (New York: Vintage Books, 1988) p. 191.
9. Martin Rees, *Our Cosmic Habitat* (Princeton: University Press, 2001) ch. 1.
* Page references to Plato and Aristotle are those customarily used, and indicated in the margins of vitually all editions.

Chapter Eight

The Understanding of Creation in Islamic Thought: A Response to Keith Ward

M.B. Altaie

Prof Altaie has already been introduced to readers, in the pre-amble to Chapter Two. In his second Islamic response, he challenges Prof Ward's contention that the essentials of Thomas Aquinas's view of the God-world relation are truly common to the three Abrahamic faiths. In counterweight to this claim, he sketches a modern, scientific interpretation of the Kalām – the over-arching philosophical-theological standpoint of early Qur'anic thinkers. In particular, he is sympathetic to the Mutakallimūn, who strove almost from the outset of the Muslim era, and crucially before the assimilation of Greek ideas, for a rational formulation of Qur'anic concepts.

Prof Ward considers two interpretations of the concept of creation in the Abrahamic faiths. (By the term "creation" I take him to mean the existence of this intelligible world). The first is what he calls the "classical" view, formulated most completely by Thomas Aquinas, but originally based on Greek philosophies, mainly those of Plato and Aristotle. The second is the modern "relational" view, which is based on the Idealistic philosophy of Hegel and the Process philosophy of Whitehead.

One of the main points of my response to Ward is his claim that the classical Thomistic view was shared between all the Abrahamic faiths. I will try to show that, as far as Islam is concerned, this claim is inaccurate. I will present the dominant Islamic view of creation and the existence of this intelligible world. My second point of response will be concerned with the general understanding in the Abrahamic faiths of the creator God as a personal entity. Due to the limited space here I will only briefly criticize this concept of a personal God and I will try to show that this type of understanding is no longer compatible with modern scientific understanding of the cosmos and the laws that govern it.

The "Classical" view

The Bible did not provide a clear basis for philosophical contemplation, enabling one to define an original view of creation, other than saying that the cosmos was created in six days by a perfect spiritual being, from whom all things issue and to whom all things return. For this reason, Christianity found no alternative but to resort to Greek philosophies in its search for guidance in understanding creation and life. Considering the environment of its early growth, adoption of Greek philosophy by the Christian Church was inevitable.

The thesis of this classical view is based on the assumption of the existence of God, the being with maximal knowledge, power, and happiness. Essentially, God was taken as a personal entity with some superior attributes. The basis on which the divine attributes are deduced in the Thomistic view stems from the Aristotelian differentiation between the perfect and the corrupt. This originally goes back to the literature of Mesopotamia in which heaven was regarded as the place for the Gods and considered to be the perfect. However, the almost mystical way in which we view what we designate as perfect influences our deductions so as to make us feel that some results are reasonable when they are not logically necessary. In this respect I would point to the concepts "goodness" and "happiness" which are used by Prof Ward. These two terms are not found in the Qur'an, probably because they are relative concepts which cannot be ascribed an absolute meaning.

The view presented in the first part of Prof Ward's paper is actually the Christian belief as formulated by Thomas Aquinas. I question whether we can say that this view is representative of the Abrahamic faiths in general. The Islamic view differs from that presented in several fundamental respects. The first is the way Muslims understand God and the divine attributes. The second is the way Muslims understand the doctrine of the creation and its connections with other properties of the world.

The attributes of God

In Ward's account, the consciousness of God plays a central role in our understanding of creation and conception of the relationship between God and the world. By contrast, the Qur'an does not say that Allah is conscious, but rather that he is living or alive and is powerful enough to sustain all the creation (*Qayuoom*). The attributes of God are some aspects that have been designated in the Qur'an as pertaining to God and as resembling the analogous aspects of humans.[1] However, it is widely agreed among Muslims that these attributes are not to be taken literally but metaphorically. The Qur'an clearly states that nothing resembles God "Naught is as His likeness; and He is the Hearer, the Seer" (Q: 43, 11). Nevertheless, the description of God given in the Holy Scriptures of all the three Abrahamic faiths is essentially personal.

This description has restricted the understanding of God and his actions and provokes some questions regarding the feelings of God toward the events that take place in our world. For example we ask whether God suffers or whether he gets sad or happy as a result of human actions. Then we puzzle whether God experiences suffering and whether he is to be considered responsible for the sufferings of humans since, in his omnipotence, he could prevent them ... and so on. I regard this kind of understanding of God as outdated: it is an understanding which may have been suitable until the end of the nineteenth century, but never after. To know that there is neither absolute space nor absolute time – that instead space and time are actually interwoven into one entity called spacetime – and hence to discover the relation between mass and energy; to know that physical measurement involves an inherent uncertainty, so that laws of nature are not necessarily deterministic but are probabilistic; and to know that countless other worlds might possibly exist beyond our perception and comprehension ... All this is surely something that ought to enhance our understanding of God? I do not understand why we should limit ourselves to an understanding of God which assumes personal character. A personal God may be necessary for the iconic vision of religion, rather than this more abstract self-transcendent understanding, but surely the latter is a more developed concept?

Part of what is called the classical view of creation was already criticized in the 12th century CE by al-Ghazālī, in his famous book, *The incoherence of the philosophers*.[2] He showed that philosophers who adopted Greek views were unsuccessful in achieving a coherent theory of divine attributes and divine action.

Before al-Ghazālī the defense of religious Islamic doctrines was undertaken by the Mutakallimūn. These were groups of Muslim thinkers with theological backgrounds who appeared during the 8th century CE and remained active until around the 12th century, when they were abandoned by the then Caliph for socio-political reasons. Mutakallimūn were interested in constructing an Islamic understanding of God, humanity and the world through rational interpretation drawn from the original Islamic sources, mainly the Qur'an. Kalām was a main-stream line of thought that was practised by Mutakallimūn and originally devised to defend Islamic religious beliefs. In fact, Muslim religious belief never came into full agreement with Greek philosophy, despite the efforts of philosophers like al-Farabi in the 9th century, Avicenna (11th) and Averroes (12th) to reconcile philosophy and Islam. The works of these philosophers were received with caution by contemporary Muslim clerics and later strongly refuted by al-Ghazālī. The true Islamic view is actually expressed in the views of the Mutakallimūn, whose thinking was not influenced by Greece. Recent works on Kalām have supported the contention that this phase of Islamic thought contains the most genuine Islamic views of God, humanity, and nature.[3] In fact, Greek philosophy was only employed by the Christian Church in defence of its beliefs, and was then adopted to stand for the Christian worldview. Jews, like mainstream Muslims, do not seem to have taken much from the Greeks.

In my view the real conflict between theistic and atheistic views stems from the atheist's difficulty in accepting a personal God. This is a legitimate objection; it is reasonable to say that the notion of a personal God is to some extent an influence of our own existence and character. However, this influence is unavoidable, and has to some extent forced us to characterize God as a person, otherwise his character would be difficult to conceive. Nevertheless, I think the time has come to realize that God is not a strictly personal being despite his personal attributes. In the same sense what we term "perfect" is actually a product of our own extrapolations. I think we ought to redefine the terms we use in ways that would enable us to use them in multi-contextual places. The personalized attributes of God make him limited and temporal and this may make the very concept of God seem incoherent.

To say that the physical cosmos is one actualization of a set of possible states that exist in the mind of God, that the actualization takes place because of an evaluation of those possible states by God, and that they are actualized for the sake of their value or goodness, is mostly a Christian theological view of the situation. The Qur'an clearly indicates that creation is realized for a purpose; this purpose is to actualize a high-ranking state of consciousness through development from a primitive state. To my understanding, creation seems to be an exercise by which a reasonably high-ranking creature is developed with some primary capabilities that enable him to comprehend the universe in which he lives. Through such comprehension and through long struggle and wrestling with nature he may get to the state where he can fully comprehend God and then unite with him. For this purpose the universe is deemed to be comprehensible, evil becomes a necessity to provoke good deeds and avoid bad ones, and punishment and reward are required in order to develop the self-competence of this creature. Through the ages we get to know God better and more accurately until we attain union with him. Such a goal might be approached through evolutionary progress. However it cannot be fully realized within our physical existence, but only when we become part of him.

This may not be, in all its details, the classical Islamic view, but I find in it no contradictions with the approach of the Mutakallimūn or the stipulations of the Qur'an.

Does God suffer?

To say that God is unaware of the suffering of the cosmos would be incompatible with his omniscience. To say that God is transcendent, so does not participate in the imperfect material world, is completely unjustified since he has already created this imperfect material world in the first place. So should he not participate in the development of the world or should we say that once he created the world he retired, leaving the world to develop on its own? I think that Aristotle was consistent when he assumed God to be a "prime mover" but then the question arises as to who sustains the world? The development of the world needs the operation and coordination of the laws of nature. Modern quantum theory indicates the necessity for a controller and a coordinator to make this world possible; I mean the necessity for an agent who would put fire into the equations and choose between the contingencies. Who can do such a job other than God? I think we should agree that modern science has surpassed all the arguments put forward by Aristotle and Plato; we need to consider a new logic and a new vision of the world. Below I will show that this serious problem of having the perfect being influencing the imperfect material world was solved already within Islamic Kalām through the principle of re-creation.

God is not an ordinary person so he does not need to have empathetic knowledge. God is in no need of simulations; he is the all-knowing omniscient and omnipotent that exists outside and inside our world, and he is an entity which no longer can be pointed to in a naive personal way.

True God cannot be altered by things that happen in the universe, but we should note that it is not necessary for God to experience a change in order to know what is happening in the universe. Rather, the divine power is wholly creative and, to actualize this, the world has to be re-created every moment, as I will explain below.

It is clear through direct observation that this universe is built to follow nearly fixed algorithms and has been established as such in order to be comprehensible. The intelligibility of the universe is necessary for us to comprehend God. We do this by realizing the beauty of the design and consequently perceive the purpose behind creation. Divine action in the world need not comply with our hopes and wishes for the good reason that our wishes and preferences may well contradict established algorithms that are necessary for the existence and development of the world. If the established algorithms were to disappear this would make the universe unintelligible, so that it looked completely random.

The multiverse proposal

The proposal of a multiverse is only a theoretical suggestion; it has nothing necessarily to do with reality. In a proper quantum vision, I think the components of a multiverse may have to be mutually orthogonal in order to be consistent with the framework of quantum theory. In this case only one state of the universe could actualize. However, the question still remains as to who has decided that this possible universe should exist rather than another, or nothing at all. One may argue that life has developed here on planet Earth, whereas there are many other planets that cannot accommodate life. The very existence of the many lifeless planets is suggestive of the existence of many lifeless universes. However, a counter argument will say that the non-existence of life on other planets is actually due to the fact that the conditions for life to exist are very subtle and sensitive. Having all other planets abiding by the same laws of physics would cause the planet on which life exists to be distinctive. But should different planets obey different laws of physics we could not then justify the non-existence of life on those planets. Similarly, a multiverse theory should require all other hypothetical universes to abide by the same laws that apply in our universe; otherwise we could not say why life should not exist in them. However, no strong scientific argument exists which can confirm that the other hypothetical universes do follow the same laws of physics as ours; to the contrary the hypothesis of a multiverse is often used to justify the accurate selection of a set of laws that have made life possible on Earth.

The Islamic views of Atomism and Re-Creation

In its most simple and direct form the Islamic view of creation is what the Qur'an says about it. To some extent this is what is basically shared with Judaism and Christianity. However the Qur'an contains some details concerning the development and fate of the universe, and the heavenly bodies like sun, moon, and stars, which cannot be found in the Bible.[4] In its most sophisticated form, the Islamic view of creation is best represented by the works of Mutakallimūn.[5] Mutakallimūn presented a comprehensive theory of God, humanity and the world that can very well stand as representing the trends of genuine Islamic thought. By contrast, the works of philosophers like al-Farabi, Avicenna, and Averroes cannot be judged in these terms since they followed the approaches of the Greeks and adopted most of their arguments.

The most prominent of the principles of Kalām were atomism and re-creation. By adopting the principle of atomism, taken in a very broad sense, Mutakallimūn identified the building blocks of the creation; then, by the principle of re-creation, they justified all the foreseen and the unforeseen properties of this creation. Indeed, the most elegant proposal of Kalām was this principle of re-creation, by which the world is assumed to be in a state of sustained re-creation at every single moment of time. This principle was devised as an essential part of the Kalām theory of atomism, according to which every body (or every entity like the soul) is assumed to be composed of "atoms" and "accidents". The Islamic atom is an abstract entity that acts as a substrate for the accidents. The accidents define the properties of the body and whatever attributes that body may acquire. The majority of Mutakallimūn assumed that the accidents were not fixed but ever-changing, in a continual process of re-creation. They proposed this in order to preserve the involvement of God in the world and to perform his essential role, which they saw as necessary (but not always sufficient) to sustain the existence of the world. Mutakallimūn couldn't see any chance for the existence of the world without the continued involvement of and sustaining by God. The reason was that nature in their view cannot act on its own because it has no will, no mind, and no ability to discern and coordinate different contingencies. This assumption led Mutakallimūn to conclude that nature must be indeterminate, and consequently led them to deny the existence of a natural deterministic causality. This principle of the Kalām sets the concept of creation in its operational meaning.

When we revisit the assumption of continual re-creation we find it to be a very profound description of a basic law that is needed to explain some findings of modern physics and, at the same time, is capable of resolving some basic theological paradoxes such as the one concerning how the absolute perfect being can influence the imperfect material world. The direct answer to this is that if the perfect being has created the imperfect world once, the continued re-creation of the world will establish continued contact and influence in much the same way as when it was first created.

Time, according to Mutakallimūn, is discrete (i.e. it, too, is atomized, like matter). It is a renewable entity and is a measure or indicator of change.[6] The timelessness of God in his frame of reference is reflected as a temporality of our world through re-creation. Through this process the timeless being God can be in continual contact with the temporal world.

The Kalām principle of re-creation has some profound physical implications too. It can explain why we should have many possible states for a physical object, why we have probability values of quantum states rather than one single instantaneous measured value, and why the world should be indeterministic. Re-creation of a physical measurable, say the position of a body x, will entail a change of the system with respect to this x. This change will affect the value of x itself and consequently will make us unable to determine the exact position of the body. Viewed in its mathematical form this can be represented by acting on the system with an operator x and then acting immediately with the derivative operator with respect to x (i.e., with the generator of a translation) which is known to represent the momentum of the body. The continued re-creation will then establish an inherent uncertainty in measuring variables of this sort, which are called "complementary variables". Again in the mathematical description the existence of the uncertainty in the measured values stems from the non-commutability of the variable and the change of the system with respect to that variable. Should there be no change there will be no uncertainty. This is why quantum indeterminacy is a dynamical characteristic in which the process of re-creation plays the most profound role. In formal quantum theory all of this is presented by the wave-mechanical description of the physical systems which I find to be compatible with the re-creation description.

Notes and References

1. In the Qur'an, divine attributes are called the "Good Names of Allah". Terming these attributes "names" is a very accurate way to describe the fact that their meanings are intended to designate a quality rather than expressing the true content of the attributes.
2. Al-Ghazālī, *The Incoherence of the Philosophers*, English translation by Michael Marmura (Utah: Brigham Young University Press, 2000).

3. H. Wolfson, *The Philosophy of the Kalām* (Harvard: University Press, 1976). H.M. Al-Alousī, *The Problem of Creation in Islamic Thought: Qur'an, Hadith, Commentaries and Kalām* (Baghdad: National Printing and Publishing Co., 1968). Also see his Ph.D. thesis submitted to Cambridge University, 1965; W.L. Craig, *The Kalām Cosmological Argument* (London: Macmillan, 1979); A. Dhanani, *The Physical Theory of Kalām: Atoms, Space, and time in Basrian Mu'tazili Cosmology* (Leiden: Brill, 1994); M.B. Altaie, "The Scientific value of Daqiq al-Kalām", *Journal of Islamic Thought and Scientific Creativity* 4 (1994) pp. 7-18.
4. See my response to David Wilkinson's paper, Ch. 2 of this volume.
5. Wolfson, ref.3, Chapter V.
6. M. B. Altaie, *Time in Islamic Kalām*, short paper delivered at the conference on "Einstein, God and Time" at the Ian Ramsey Centre, Oxford, Sept. 12-15, 2005.

Chapter Nine

Judaism and Creation

Dan Cohn-Sherbok

Prof Dan Cohn-Sherbok was born in the US, and initially studied there. He subsequently obtained a PhD from Cambridge (England) and a DD from Hebrew Union College, New York. He taught theology for a number of years at the University of Kent, before moving to his current position as Professor of Judaism at the University of Wales, Lampeter. He has written or edited over 80 books, several of them with his wife, Lavinia. Recent titles include "Interfaith Theology: a Reader" (Oneworld, 2002), "Judaism: History, Belief and Practice" (Taylor & Francis, 2003) and "Vision of Judaism: Wrestling with God" (Continuum, 2004).

The text which follows was intended for a plenary session for the 2006 conference. In the event, Prof Cohn-Sherbok was unable to deliver it at the time. However, its account, both personal and authoritative, of Jewish thinking from the earliest period to the confrontation with 21st C cosmology, makes a pivotal contribution to this volume.

For the Jewish people, the belief in creation is of central importance. God is the source of all things, and this doctrine is celebrated throughout the year in the liturgy. In rabbinic literature, the biblical narrative served as the basis for considerable speculation. This was particularly acute in mystical sources, where attempts were made to penetrate the meaning of creation. In the history of Jewish philosophy, speculation about the nature of creation also played a central role. Today, religious Jews continue to uphold this belief, yet the findings of modern science have challenged the biblical account of the origin of the universe.

Growing Up with the Creation Account

My religious education in a Reform synagogue in the United States was grounded in the Hebrew Bible. In the first years of religion school, our teachers recited to us the biblical account of creation. For six days, we were told, God created the Heavens and the Earth. "In the beginning," they read, "God created the heavens and the earth. The earth was without form and void, and darkness was upon the face of the deep; and the Spirit of God was moving over the face of the waters." Then God created light. God saw that the light was good; He separated the light from the darkness. Then he called the light day and the darkness night. This completed his creative work for the first day. On the second day He formed the firmament in the midst of the waters, thereby creating heaven. On the third day, the dry land and vegetation were made. God said: "Let the earth put forth vegetation, plants yielding seed, and fruit trees bearing fruit in which is their seed, each according to its kind." On the fourth day God placed lights in the firmament in the heavens. He then proceeded to create birds and fish and He blessed them, saying: "Be fruitful and multiply and fill the waters in the seas, and let birds multiply on the earth."

Finally, on the sixth day, God bestowed life on animals and human beings. Quoting from the second chapter of Genesis, they explained that Adam was placed in the Garden of Eden where God commanded him to refrain from eating from the tree of the knowledge of good and evil: "The Lord God took the man and put him in the garden of Eden to till it and keep it. And the Lord God commanded the man saying, 'You may freely eat of every tree of the garden; but of the tree of the knowledge of good and evil you shall not eat, for in the day that you eat of it you shall die.' The Lord then created Eve as a helper for him, for as He said: 'It is not good that the man should be alone'." Eve, too, was told that she was free to eat from all the trees of the garden except for the tree that He had forbidden to Adam.

Although in ordinary school we had been taught scientific theories about the origin of the universe and the evolution of human beings, we did not question the biblical narrative. Instead, we listened to the story of creation and accepted it as an essential part of the Jewish heritage. In the natural history museum in the city where I grew up I had seen prehistoric creatures. I knew that the universe was millions of years old. But I never puzzled over the biblical account. Admittedly, it seemed implausible that Adam and Eve could have been historical figures who were tricked by a wily serpent into eating forbidden fruit. But I did not challenge the claim that God was the creator of the universe. This seemed entirely believable.

Every Saturday morning in synagogue, the rabbi repeated this belief in the worship service. God, we heard, had created all things, and we were encouraged to acknowledge his power over nature. At the end of the service, he quoted the traditional prayer of praise from the *Amidah*:

> Praised be Thou, O Lord our God, Ruler of the world, who in Thy mercy makest light to shine over the earth, and all its inhabitants, and renewest daily the work of creation. How manifold are Thy works, O Lord! In wisdom hast Thou made them all. The heavens declare Thy glory. The earth reveals Thy creative power. Thou formest light and darkness, ordainest good out of evil, bringest harmony into nature and peace to the heart of man.
>
> Thou didst lay the foundations of the earth and the heavens are Thy handiwork. They may perish but Thou shalt endure. The heavens shall have no end. O everliving God, Creator of heaven and earth, rule Thou over us forever. Praised be Thou, O Lord, Creator of light. [1]

God's creation of the universe was directly linked to Sabbath observance. Just as God had rested on the seventh day, so we too were told to remember the Sabbath. Lifting the wine cup, the rabbi recited the *Kiddush* prayer:

> Praised be Thou, O Lord our God, Ruler of the world, who hast created the fruit of the vine. Praised be Thou, O Lord our God, King of the Universe, who hast sanctified us with Thy commandments. In love hast Thou given us, O Lord Our God, the holy Sabbath as a heritage, a remembrance of creation. For that day is the prologue to the Exodus from Egypt. For us did you choose and us did you sanctify from all the nations. And your holy Sabbath, with love and favour did you give us as a heritage. Blessed are you, O Lord, our God, who sanctifies the Sabbath. [2]

Thus within Reform Judaism – as in the other major modern Jewish movements – the belief in God's creation is of supreme importance. Despite the discoveries of modern science, Reform Jews join with their coreligionists in proclaiming with faith that God alone formed the universe, and rules over it in glory.

One Creator

From biblical times to the present, Jews have affirmed that God is the source of all things. In the Hebrew Bible, the term *bore* (Creator) is frequently used to describe God. In the traditional synagogue, a hymn recited before readings from the Psalms stresses that before God's creative act nothing existed: "Blessed be He who spake, and the world existed; Blessed be He; Blessed be He who was the Master of the world at the beginning." [3]

Another synagogue hymn emphasizes God's eternal nature: "Thou wast the same before the world was created; Thou hast been the same since the world hath been created." [4] The *Ani Maamin* (I believe) prayer, formulated in the sixteenth century, echoes this theme:

> I believe with perfect faith that the Creator, blessed be His name, is the Author and Guide of everything that has been created, and that He alone has made, does make, and will make all things. 5

According to the twelfth-century Jewish philosopher, Maimonides, the belief in creation is one of the thirteen basic principles of Judaism. Unlike everything else, whose existence is contingent on God's creative action, He alone necessarily exists:

> The foundation of all foundations and the pillar of wisdom is to know that there is a First Being. He it is who brought all things into being and all beings in heaven and in between only enjoy existence by virtue of His true being. If it could be imagined that He does not exist, nothing else could have existed. But if it could be imagined that no other beings, apart from Him, enjoyed existence, He alone would still exist and He could not cease because they have ceased. For all beings need Him but He, blessed be He, does not need them, not any of them. Consequently, His true nature is different from the truth regarding any of them. [6]

In rabbinic literature, the sages speculated about the nature of the creative process. Drawing on the Platonic concept of the idea of the world in the mind of God, *Genesis Rabbah* (*midrash* on Genesis), for example, asserts that God looked into the Torah and created the cosmos. [8] Here the Torah is conceived as a primordial blueprint of creation. Regarding the order of creation, in the first century C.E. the School of Shammai stated: "The heavens were created first and then the earth" (following Genesis 1:1). The School of Hillel, however, maintained that heaven and earth were created at the same time.[9] In the same century, a philosopher said to Rabban Gamaliel: "Your God is a great craftsman, but he found good materials to help him in the work of creation, namely *tohu* and *vohu*, darkness, spirit, water and the deep." In reply, Rabban Gamaliel quoted other biblical verses to illustrate that these materials were themselves created by God.[10] In the third century R. Johanan stated that God took two coils, one of fire and the other of snow, wove them into each other, and created the universe.[11] According to another rabbinic source, all things were formed simultaneously on the first day of creation, but appeared on the other six days just as figs are gathered in one basket but each is selected individually.[12] Again, in *Genesis Rabbah* the sages emphasize that God formed several worlds, but destroyed them before creating this one.[13] The goal of creation is summed up in the rabbinic claim that whatever the Holy One, blessed be He, created in his world, He did this for his glory.[14] In early mystical texts, Jewish sages propounded other theories concerning the nature of the creative process. In the *Sefer Yetsirah* (Book of Creation) – the earliest mystical cosmological tract – God is described as creating the universe by means of the letters of the Hebrew alphabet. According to this text, God hewed them, combined them, weighed them, interchanged them, and through them produced the whole creation and everything that is destined to come into being. These letters are of three types: mothers, doubles and singles. The mothers (*shin, mem, aleph*) symbolize the three primordial elements of all existing things; they represent in the microcosm (the human form), the head, the belly and the chest. In addition to these three mother letters, there are seven double letters (*beth, gimel, daleth, caph, peh, resh, tau*) which signify the contraries in the universe. These letters were formed, designed, created and combined into the stars of the universe, the days of the week, and the orifices of perception in human beings. Finally, there are twelve simple letters (*he, vav, zayin, chet, tet, yod, lamed, nun, samek, ayin, tsade,* and *kof*) which correspond to the chief activities – sight, hearing, smell, speech, desire for food, the sexual appetite, movement, anger, mirth, thought, sleep and work. These letters are also emblematic of the twelve signs of the zodiac in the heavenly sphere, the twelve months, and the chief limbs of the body. Thus, human beings, world, and time are linked to one another through the process of creation.

These recondite doctrines are supplemented in the *Sefer Yetsirah* by a theory of emanation. The first *sefirah* (divine emanation) is the spirit of the living God; air is the second of the *sefirot* and is derived from the first. On it are hewn the twenty-two Hebrew letters. The third *sefirah* is the water that comes from the air. The fourth of the *sefirot* is the fire which comes from water through which God made the heavenly wheels, the seraphim and the ministering angels. The remaining six *sefirot* are the six dimensions of space. These ten *sefirot* are the moulds into which all created things were originally cast. They constitute form rather than matter. The twenty-two letters, on the other hand, are the prime cause of matter: everything that exists is due to their creative force, but they receive their form from the *sefirot*. According to this cosmological doctrine, God transcends the universe; nothing exists outside of him. The visible world is the result of the emanation of the divine. By combining emanation and creation in this manner, the *Sefer Yetsirah* attempts to harmonize the concept of divine immanence and transcendence. God is immanent in that the *sefirot* are an outpouring of his spirit, and he is transcendent in that the matter which was shaped into the forms is the product of his creative action.

In the Middle Ages, a number of Jewish theologians believed that god created the universe *ex nihilo*. The kabbalists (Jewish mystics), however, interpreted the doctrine of *ex nihilo* in a special sense. God, they argued, should be understood as the Divine Nothing because as He is in and of himself, nothing can be predicated. The Divine is beyond human understanding. As the *Zohar* (the thirteenth-century mystical text) explains, God as Infinite (*Ayn Sof*) is beyond human comprehension:

> Master of the worlds, you are the cause of causes, the first cause who waters the tree with a spring; this spring is like the soul to the body, since it is like the life of the body. In you there is no image, nor likeliness of what is within, nor of what is without...There is none that knows anything of you, and besides you there is no singleness or unity in the upper or the lower worlds. You are acknowledged as Lord over all. As for all the *sefirot*, each one has a known name and you are the perfect completion of them all. When you remove yourself from them, all the names are left like a body without a soul. [15]

Creation *ex nihilo*, therefore, refers to the creation of the universe out of God, the Divine Nothing. Embracing the theory of emanation in earlier sources such as the *Sefer Yetsirah*, kabbalists argued that this occurred through a series of divine emanations. In their view, the first verses of Genesis allude to the processes within the Godhead prior to the creation of the universe. Following the teaching of Isaac Luria in the sixteenth century, later Jewish mystics understood the notion of God creating and destroying worlds before the creation of this world as referring to spiritual worlds. Thus *tohu* (void) in Genesis denotes the stage of God's self-revelation known as *olam ha-tohu* (world of the void) which precedes *olam ha-tikkun* (world of perfection). Other kabbalists, such as the Hasidic scholar Kalonymous Kalman of Cracow, maintained that the void in Genesis is the primordial void remaining after God's withdrawal to make room for the universe (*tzimtzum*). On this reading, God's decree, "Let there be light" (Genesis 1:3), means that God caused his light to emanate into the void in order to provide sustaining power required for the worlds which were later to be formed. [16]

Regarding the question whether, in the process of creating the comsos, God also created intelligent beings on other planets, the Bible offers no information. Even though rabbinic sources attest to the creation of other worlds, they similarly contain no reference to the existence of other sentient creatures. In the nineteenth century, however, Phineas Elijah ben Meir Hurwitz of Vilna discussed this issue. On the basis of Isaiah 45:18 ("For thus says the Lord who created the heavens [He is God!], who formed the earth and made it, He established it; He did not create it a chaos; He formed it to be inhabited: 'I the Lord; and there is no other!'"), he maintained that there are creatures on other planets than the earth. In this connection he referred to a passage in the Talmud[17] in which *Meroz* (Judges 5:23) is a star. Since it is cursed, Hurwitz concluded that it is inhabited. He alleged that creatures on other planets may have intelligence, yet he did not think they would have free will since only human beings have such capacity. Therefore, he wrote, "there is only room for Torah and worship in this world; they would have no place where free will is absent."[18]

In a modern discussion of this issue, the Reform rabbi Gunther Plaut asks:

> Will the possibility that there are intelligent creatures on other planets impose any strain on our religious beliefs?... The modern Jew will answer this question with a firm "No." An earlier generation, rooted in beliefs in an earth-centred universe, might have had some theological difficulties, but we have them no longer...Just as a father may love many children with equal love, so surely may our Father on high spread his pinions over the vastness of creation.[19]

An alternative Jewish view has been advanced by the Orthodox rabbi Norman Lamm. There are, he believes, three major challenges confronting Judaism. The existence of extraterrestrial beings underlies the conviction that human beings are the ultimate purpose of God's creation. The second challenge relates to the generation of life. If life is generated by natural processes on other planets, how is one to understand the doctrine of God as Creator? The final challenge concerns the temptation to view God in non-personal terms given this new vision of the universe. Lamm believes that Judaism is able to resolve these difficulties. He concludes: "We may yet learn that, as rational, sentient, and self-conscious creatures, 'we are not alone.' But then again we never felt before nor need we feel today or in the future that we are alone, 'For Thou art with me'."[20]

The Jewish scholar Louis Jacobs points out that the challenges Lamm mentions are not the crucial ones. The most serous difficulty is the question of the uniqueness of the Torah:

Lamm's arguments center around what the Torah means in the light of the new possible situation. But if this possibility is real, the far more difficult and radical question to be faced is that there are whole worlds for which the Torah, given to humans, can have no meaning. In asking what Judaism has to say about extraterrestrial life, Lamm begs the question whether Judaism has any relevance in this context.[21]

Leaving aside this debate about the existence of extra-terrestrial life, there is no doubt that the belief that God is the source of all continues to animate Jewish religious sensibilities. Maimonides' formulation of this principle in the beginning of his Code expresses what has remained the central feature of the Jewish religious system:

The foundation of all foundations and the pillar of wisdom is to know that there is a First Being. He it is who brought all things into being and all the beings in the heaven and earth and in between only enjoy existence by [him].[22]

Science and Creation

The biblical account in the Book of Genesis was written in a pre-scientific age. Hence, it is not surprising that the depiction of the creation of the universe conflicts in numerous respects with the findings of modern science. According to Scripture, God created the world in six days and rested on the seventh. The verb *bara* used in Genesis 1:1 does not imply creation *ex nihilo*, but denotes a process whereby God utilized various primordial elements in creating the cosmos. The opening sentence begins with the temporal clause: "When God began to create the heaven and the earth," and continues with a reference to darkness and void. The first creative act was the formation of light: "And God said, 'Let there be light,' and there was light." (Gen. 1:2)

The six days of creation are divided into a symmetrical pattern of three days each, in which the creation of light and of day and night occurred on the first day, the sky on the second, and dry land, seas and vegetation on the third. Then follow the creation of luminaries on the fourth day, living creatures of the sea and sky on the fifth, and land animals and human beings on the sixth. Throughout it is stressed that "God saw that it was good, and there was evening and there was morning" – this is followed by the completion of each day's labour. The final act of the creation of Adam is preceded by a declaration of God's purpose announced in the heavenly council: "Let us make man in our image, after our likeness." (Gen. 1:26) Adam is then blessed by God and told to be fertile, increase the earth, and master it. He is entrusted with sovereignty over the fish of the sea, the birds of the sky, and all living things that creep on earth (Gen. 1:28) In the second account of creation in chapter 2, a much more anthropocentric version is given of God's dealings with Adam and Eve.

What are we to make of the biblical narrative? For centuries, Jews have viewed this account of creation as literally true. Even within the various progressive branches of Judaism, it is accepted as an accurate picture of God's activity. As the source of all things, God formed the heavens and earth in six days, but rested on the seventh. For this reason, the Jewish people are commanded to rest on the Sabbath day from all their labours. Yet, modern science provides a totally different account of the development of the cosmos and the origin of life. Today there is widespread agreement among scientists that the cosmos was formed through a big bang. Scientists explain that, as the world emerged the spatial order was formed; then space boiled in the rapid expansion of the inflationary era, blowing the universe apart with rapidity. The perfect symmetry of the original structure was later broken as the cooling brought about by expansion crystallized out the forces of nature. For some time, the universe was a hot soup of quarks and gluons and leptons, but by the time it was one ten-thousandth of a second old, this age of transformations ceased and matter took the form of protons, neutrons and electrons.

At this point, the entire cosmos was hot enough to be the arena of nuclear reactions which continued for three minutes. The gross nuclear structure was then left at a quarter helium and three-quarters hydrogen. It was then far too hot for atoms to form around these nuclei – this would not occur for half a million years. By then the universe had become cool enough for matter and radiation to separate. The world then suddenly became transparent and a sea of radiation was left to continue cooling. Gravity was the dominant force in the next area of cosmic history. This continued its battle against the original expansive tendency of the big bang, stopping the universe from being too dilute, but failing to bring about an implosive collapse. Even though the universe was nearly uniform at that stage, small fluctuations were present, producing sites at which there was excess matter. The effect of gravity enhanced these irregularities until, after about a billion years, the universe began to become lumpy and the galaxies and their stars began to form.

Within the stars, nuclear reactions began and the contractive force of gravity heated up the stellar cores beyond their ignition temperature. Hydrogen was "burned" to become helium, and eventually a delicate chain of nuclear reactions started which generated further energy and the heavier elements up to iron. After a life of ten billion years, stars began to die. Some were so constituted that they did this in supernova explosions. This resulted in the dissemination of the elements into the wider environment; at the same time, the heavier elements beyond iron were produced in reactions with the high energy neutrinos blowing off the outer envelopes of exploding stars.

As more stars and planets condensed, the conditions of chemical composition, temperature, and radiation led to the next new development in cosmic history. Perhaps half a billion years after conditions on earth became favourable, long chain molecules formed with the power of replicating themselves. They rapidly used the chemical food in the shallow waters of early earth, and the three billion years of the history of life commenced. A genetic code was established, and primitive unicellular entities transformed the atmosphere of earth from one containing carbon dioxide to one containing oxygen. The process of photosynthesis evolved, and eventually life began to become more complex. About seven hundred million years ago, jellyfish and worms were the most advanced life forms. About three hundred and fifty million years ago, life moved from the sea onto dry land, and seventy million years ago, dinosaurs disappeared. Three and a half million years ago, Australopithecines began to walk erect; *homo sapiens* appeared two-three hundred thousand years ago.

The clash between these two rival views of the origin of the cosmos illustrates the archaic nature of biblical speculation about the beginning of all things. For the writers of Scripture, God is at the centre of this process: He is the source of all that exists. Modern scientists, on the other hand, are concerned to explain in physical terms the sequence of events that took place when the universe was formed. Basing their conclusions on physical, chemical and biological evidence, they have provided a coherent picture of the process by which the cosmos came into being. Despite efforts made by contemporary theologians to reconcile the biblical narrative with modern scientific theory, it is obvious that the authors of Genesis had a limited understanding of the true nature of the origin of the cosmos. The Bible's presentation of events is wholly inaccurate. This is true as well of the kabbalistic understanding of divine emanation and the formation of the cosmos by means of letter combination. These theories are nothing more than mystical speculation based on unfounded religious presuppositions.

A new vision of Judaism calls for a re-evaluation of the Biblical story. It should now be recognized that the cosmological mythology of the ancient Israelites emerged out of a particular social and cultural context. Influenced by Babylonian legends, the authors of Genesis reformulated these ancient Near Eastern epics to suit their own religious purposes. For these writers, it was the God of the Israelites – not the numerous deities of Babylonian mythology – who had fashioned the universe out of primordial elements. During the six days of creation, they believed, God did all his work and rested on the seventh day. As modern Jews, however, we should set aside such unsophisticated notions, replacing them with a scientific understanding of the origins of the universe. In the quest to explain the true nature of reality, we can adopt modern methods of investigation and experimentation – such a Copernican shift in orientation is a precondition for the reconstruction of Judaism for the twenty-first century.

Notes and References

1. *The Union Prayerbook II*, Central Conference of American Rabbis (1961) p. 44
2. Ibid, p. 93
3. Singer, S., *Authorized Daily Prayer Book* (London, 1962) p. 17
4. Ibid, p. 10
5. Ibid, p. 93
6. Maimonides, *Yad*: *Yesode Ha-Torah*, 1:1-3
7. Terms used in this section, which may be unfamiliar to non-Jewish readers, include:
midrash (pl, *midrashim*) – a rabbinical interpretation of scripture
rabbah – collection of *midrashim* concerning a named book
Torah – generally the divine law, specifically the first five books of the Bible, which contain that law (a.k.a. Pentateuch).
8. *Genesis Rabbah*, 1:1
9. Talmud, *Hag*. 12a
10. Ref. 8, 1:9
11. Ref. 8, 10:3
12. Ref. 8, 12:4
13. Ref. 8, 9:2
14. *Mishnah*, *Avot*, 6:11
15. Dan Cohn-Sherbok, *Jewish Mysticism: An Anthology* (Oxford: Oneworld, 1995) p. 119
16. Louis Jacobs, *A Jewish Theology* (London: Darton, Longman & Todd, 1973) p. 96
17. *Talmud* – Collection of rabbinic discussions of the law dating from early centuries CE.
18. Phineas Elijah ben Meir Hurwitz, *Sefer Ha-Berit*, Part I, *Maamar* 3: in ref 15, p. 99
19. W. Gunther Plaut, *Judaism and the Scientific Spirit* (New York, 1962) pp. 36-9
20. Norman Lamm, "The Religious Implications of Extraterrestrial Life," *Tradition*, **7**, (4) – **8** (10), Winter 1965 – Spring 1966: in ref 15, p. 106
21. Jacobs, ref 15, pp. 106-7
22. Maimonides, as ref 6.

Chapter Ten

Creation: The Jewish View

Brian Fox

Brian Fox, AM, DD is the rabbi of the Menorah synagogue, Manchester. He stepped into the Sept 2006 conference at very short notice, in place of fellow Reform rabbi, Prof Cohn-Sherbok. Though Rabbi Fox's rapidly-prepared paper gave no references[1], it was valued immensely at the time, and clearly demands inclusion in this published volume, in complement to Prof Cohn-Sherbok's piece.

Rabbi Fox is emphatic that the Genesis accounts of creation constitute poetic myth about the meaning of human existence, not cosmological science. He shows that the range of rabbinical and Talmudic thought about these myths is immense, and the divergences huge – not least about whether creation was from nothing (c.f. Dr Bonting's paper, Chap 4). Similarly, modern Judaism confronts other challenges entirely familiar to Christians, including those from both scientific and Creationist sides.

By way of introduction it is tempting for me to spend the allotted time in doing just what Biblical Judaism does: sing the praises of Creation. "The heaven reveals the glory of God and the Earth His handiwork" said the Psalmist. To which many have responded "Jews don't analyse the creation, we celebrate it."

Yet Judaism goes beyond praise. There is a significant body of literature from the medieval ages to our own time that is either more Aristotelian than Aristotle, or transforms Aquinas or out-Platos Plato. Sometimes Jewish thought says "If you want to know about creation go and ask Aristotle." At other times we are instructed to say a special prayer on meeting anyone of the calibre of a Nobel Prize winner. It is as if we are saying "There is truth out there and it is not only the property of Jews."

Science and Genesis

Starting in the Book of Genesis and echoing throughout the Hebrew Scriptures are two claims about creation:
  i) The earth is the centre of the Universe, and
  ii) The laws of nature can be altered by God's will.

If they are so, why would scientists bother to even consider such unscientific, antiquated and therefore irrelevant myths as the six days of creation, Adam and Eve and the Garden of Eden?

Of course, if Genesis were the source of scientific "truth" the scientists of our age, 3000-4000 years after Genesis, would be right. But it must be stated that Genesis is not about the scientific origins of the world and its inhabitants. It is about three very unscientific topics:
  i) God.
  ii) Human beings and their destinies, and
  iii) The relationship between that God and those human beings and their destinies.

So: are we now to exist in two separate camps, science and religion, and never the twain shall meet? I should think that the answer is NO! The creation texts in the Hebrew Scriptures have certain convictions expressed in the metaphors, the vocabulary and the world-view of antiquity. They can tell us at least three things:
  i) A particular view of human history
  ii) A particular attitude to the meaning of existence, and
  iii) A passionate expression of the role of God in history.

So, if Government needs to be told, "It's the economy stupid!" we – who derive enormous inspiration from the creation story of Genesis – would say to scientists "Lighten up! It's poetry, stupids! It is poetic truth which appeals to the imagination, the heart and the orderliness of the human mind." Or, as one Biblical scholar taught, "This God- and Israel-centred account discriminates, as every good historical narrative must, in its choice of events and presents us with history not, perhaps as it was, but as it ought to have been."

The two creation stories of Genesis

There are in fact two creation stories in Genesis. Genesis 1:1-2a dates from the 5th century B.C.E., it is from the P (Priestly) source and seems to have two goals: to have Man as the pinnacle or climax of creation and to have the Sabbath written into nature. Man ends the creation in this account: therefore value man. God rests on the Sabbath therefore *imitatio dei* (as God does, so we do) follows – we must rest on the Sabbath.

Genesis 2:4b dates from 900-750 B.C.E., is from the J (Yahwist) source and places Man at the beginning of creation along with the animals. It has an entirely different sub-text which is "Don't sin like Adam", and provides an understanding of how things began. So Adam names the animals, and we are told of the creation of woman, we are told about why we wear clothes, why serpents go on their bellies, why there is pain in childbirth and why we toil in agriculture.

How can the two creation stories be harmonised?

Anyone who has anything to do with my profession knows that an apparent contradiction in Scripture is wonderful grist to the mill for sermons. Some have said that P is about the ideal world and J the real. Some have seen an intrinsic sermon to mankind: "Strive to become the centre of the universe. You can master your inclinations. You can control nature. You can be moral, live the ethical life, care for the environment and refrain from cruelty to animals."

Because neither Genesis story deals with the question of how or when heaven, earth, darkness or void were created, there is enormous scope for conjecture. Yet at the end of the day the Biblical account leaves us with the clear message: God created an orderly and good universe.

What has Judaism said about Creation leading up to the Modern world?

So: starting with the Hebrew Scriptures, God did it and He liked what he did! "God spoke and it was done". How did it happen? Through the Divine will, by Divine fiat. This simple and direct view lasted until the first centuries after the Babylonian exile. Professor Macquarrie in a lecture in Oxford in 1971 suggested that the Hebrew approach to creation was a monarchical model as distinct from the Greek organic model. He derived that from Genesis where there is no mistake: God was the sole King/Creator and He created all the matter that he used. The Greeks were more into "process".

So: was there matter prior to creation of the world? Did God work with a moist substance? Was that matter like modelling clay? There is a huge literature in Judaism which says: perhaps there was something; while others look at *yesh may ayin*: (something from nothing) creation *ex nihilo*.

The Rabbis of the Talmudic Period

Life among the Greeks and Romans influenced Jewish thought.

Thus Rav Assi (4th Century Tiberias) said that plants were created on the third day "but did not sprout until the first man came and prayed for them".

Rabbi Judah ben Simeon (4th Century Palestine) believed that there was "an order of time that existed before the first biblical day".

Rabbi Abahu (4th Century, Palestine) believed that God created and destroyed worlds before this one. In this view he was building on Rabbi Johanan (2nd Century Palestine) who had taught that as many as 974 worlds existed before this one.

Rabbi Judah (2nd Century, Palestine) believed that man at one time had had a tail. And, finally, Rabbi Abba Kohen Bardela (2nd Century Palestine) believed that men once had "faces like monkeys".

In Hellenistic Jewish thought God was helped in creation "Let US make man in OUR image and OUR likeness" (Gen 1:26): they did not just accept the royal "We" but posited a Divine council assisting God. Building on the Divine Council, concept the Hellenists looked at Proverbs 8:1-31 and Job 28 and saw Wisdom (*chochma*) as the source of help to God in creating man and the Universe.

Philo of Alexandria 20 B.C.E.-50 C.E. was the first to marry Greek thought with Judaism when he saw the allegorical nature of the creation stories. Many Jewish philosophers built on the Aristotelian concept of creation *ex nihilo* in time (which is an ancient way of saying that at one particular moment in history there was a Big Bang).

But like everything in Jewish life (if you have two Jews you have three opinions) there are disparate views on Creation. In general Jewish philosophers have taken two paths: either to harmonize Scripture with philosophy or to defend it from Philosophy's attack when harmony was not possible. It is as if Jewish philosophers have been saying, "There can only be one truth. By definition the Scriptures are true. How therefore can we read Philosophy as if we are reading Scripture and Scripture as if we are reading Philosophy?"

Nine Philosophers who call for our attention

As we have just noted, Philo of Alexandria was able to harmonise Greek thought and Scripture through allegory. Plato had spoken of God's nature willing the universe while Philo spoke of the universe as an expression of God's choice.

Saadia Gaon (892-942 CE) was the first Jew to defend *Creatio ex nihilo* by saying that the six days of creation means that the universe is created in time. He was strident in his defence of Judaism under what he saw as an assault by Dualists, Trinitarians and Infidels.

Solomon ibn Gabirol (1020-1070) was a Neo-Platonist who believed that creation was from universal matter (not *ex nihilo*) and outside of time. He used the analogy of water from a fountain as creation without motion and without time. To ibn Gabirol, creation was a necessary emanation from God. It was he who taught that God's will led to the creation. Christian scholars have taken up this concept by connecting it with the Christian scriptures, "In the beginning was the word and the word was with God", thereby showing how the New Testament is true to the spirit of Judaism.

The moral philosopher Bahya ibn Pakuda (1050-1120) of Spain also accepted Creatio *ex nihilo*. His was the classical acceptance of the teleological and the cosmological proofs for God's existence. Creation for Bahya happened in time. When pushed to defend Scripture he simply said, "God *must* have done it!"

Judah Ha Levi (1075-1141) also of Spain said grandly "All science originated with the Jews", which was his way of saying: "You can't teach us anything!" End of discussion. Others can twist Scripture to fit in with Philosophy, but not HaLevi. For him Scripture and the Prophets are ultimate truth. Aristotle, Christianity and Islam can teach us nothing. Needless to say, HaLevi is not typical of Jewish philosophers in the middle ages.

Moses Maimonides (1135-1204) is the star among Jewish philosophers. Jews were confused as to how to marry Aristotle with scripture. Through the language of multiple significances he was able to live with both while pointing out the weaknesses in Aristotle (of which Aristotle was also aware). In his "Guide to the Perplexed" he implied the principle: *Read Scripture as if it is Aristotle and Aristotle as if it is Scripture.* Creation *ex nihilo* may have been true but it was not crucial for religious faith. He, in fact, had it both ways: he was the first Jewish philosopher to believe in *creatio ex nihilo* but Maimonides also believed that *ex nihilo* meant "from a pre-existent eternal matter". What was crucial was that creation from that "stuff" happened in time.

Karaites in Babylon-Persia (mid 8th Century CE; named "Ananites" after their founder) were literalists who believed that *creatio ex nihilo* happened in time by God. God was not created but is eternal. They completely disassociated themselves from post-Biblical thought.

Hasdai Crescas (1340-1410) worked on the edge of Judaism. He was an Aristotelian in his belief that the universe is causally dependant on God. But for Crescas God's will and God's nature are one. The universe is the product of both. He was a follower of Thomas Aquinas when he wrote that while creation in time is a true belief as taught in Genesis, it is not a fundamental belief on which Judaism either stands for falls.

Jospeh Albo (1360-144) went along with Crescas believing that Scripture is valid for all time and that the belief that *"creatio ex nihilo* happened in time" is a true belief but not a fundamental principle of Judaism. If Maimonides was the first it is true to say that Crescas and Albo were the last Jewish philosophers to defend the principle of *creatio ex nihilo*.

Other modern Jewish authors have written that, in Judaism, Man is self-creating. Creations, they believe, did not stop with Genesis. They are in good company as Rashi (10th Century CE, quoting the midrash) observed that at the end of the first creation story there is a seemingly redundant *"la a sot"* or "to do/make". So some have asked "Once creation is completed who then 'does' or 'makes'?" And the answer is "We do!" How? By learning the principles of creation, by accepting the moral responsibility and inescapable accountability inherent in the creation story, and finally, by having a broader perspective and going beyond the simple interpretation of the text. We inherited an unfinished world: we complete God's work of creating.

What of modern Judaism and Creation?

In ideology and practice all streams of modern Judaism – Humanist (man above all), Liberal (ethics above all), Reform (responsible autonomy regarding Jewish Law), Reconstructionist (redefine to avoid supernaturalism) and Conservative (traditional non-orthodox)) support scientific method while yet looking to the creation stories for inspiration. Mordechai Kaplan derived the development of the physical and social universe from Genesis. Chief Rabbi Hertz simply wrote that science and religion are about different things. The Reform movement's Rabbis wrote that the scientific method is a critical tool to help us understand ourselves. Science leading to new knowledge and new understandings of the universe can only be served by Religion's openness, desire to investigate and to learn. Not all openness to the Scientific method is confined to non-orthodox movements. The Chief Rabbi at the founding of the State of Israel, Isaac Kook, wrote "Evolution happens in spiritual matters, why not in the physical universe?"

What about creationism?

We need to define our terms: Creationism believes that the universe and all living forms came into being through the designed purpose and deliberate acts of a supernatural creator. That creator using special processes, not operating today, created stars, our solar system and all living types of plants and animals. Modern Jews would simply point out to the creationists that the methodologies of science and religion differ. Science is an open system, which works through testing, questioning and evidence-based assumptions. Religion is a closed system wherein you lose your faith if you abandon God, the world and Humanity. The Hebrew Scriptures are about morality and not cosmology. There is an implied cosmology but that is not their particular subject matter. We are about our relationships with God, and truth about life rather than scientific truths.

So what does science not address, according to Jewish thought?

Chief Rabbi Hertz asks: what of God, Man and the Universe? Others add: what of ultimacy (ultimate values)? What of moral and ethical concerns? What of ultimate priorities and ultimate meaning? Though science may embody some of these, they can never be its subject matter.

Conclusion

We are now living in a very dangerous world. The creations stories lead to one conclusion: that harmony needs to be the basis of the created world. In the beginning it all made sense. Science and religion can work together to bring order to our confusion once again.

Further reading

1. In the absence of references supplied by Rabbi Fox, the editor comments:
i) The *Encyclopaedia Judaica* (Jerusalem: Kater, 1972) has entries on all the philosophers and almost all the Talmudic rabbis mentioned by Rabbi Fox; its item on "Creation and Cosmogony" (Vol. 5, 1059-71) is also immensely informative.
ii) Shorter general works include Raphael Werblowsky and Geofrey Wigoder, eds, *The Oxford Dictionary of the Jewish Religion* (Oxford: University Press, 1997) and, substantially briefer still, Dan Cohn-Sherbok *A Concise Encyclopaedia of Judaism* (Oxford: One World. 1998).
iii) Cohn-Sherbok's *Fifty Key Jewish Thinkers* (London: Routledge, 1997 provides non-trivial discussions of all nine philosophers mentioned by Rabbi Fox.

Chapter Eleven

Cosmologies Ancient and Modern: A Response to Dan Cohn-Sherbok and Brian Fox

John Hedley Brooke

Dr. John Hedley Brooke taught the history of science at Lancaster University from 1969-1999, latterly as Professor, before moving to Oxford as the first holder of the Andreas Idreos Chair of Science & Religion, and Director of the Ian Ramsey Centre. He retired in 2006. His books include "Science and Religion: Some Historical Perspectives (Cambridge University Press, 1991); "Thinking About Matter: Studies in the History of Chemical Philosophy" (Ashgate, 1995); and (with Geoffrey Cantor) "Reconstructing Nature: The Engagement of Science & Religion" (T & T Clark, 1998). He is the current President of the Science & Religion Forum.

In this comment on the preceding papers about Jewish thought, he draws attention to points on which, despite their broadly similar attitudes, the two authors diverge; but he also notes respects in which both Christian and Islamic thinking might learn from current trends within Judaism.

In a delightful parenthesis, Rabbi Fox observes that "if you have two Jews you have three opinions". I cannot be the voice of that phantom third opinion, but it is a pleasure to reflect on the issues raised in the two preceding essays. It is instructive to be introduced to seminal Jewish thinkers who, over many centuries, have speculated not merely on the outcome of a divine creation but on the means by which it was brought about. From Professor Cohn-Sherbok we learn of Platonic conceptions finding application in the privileging of the Torah as a primordial blueprint of creation. We recognise competing images of the craftsman working with pre-existing matter and of creation *ex nihilo*. In some models creation results from a divine emanation, safeguarding God's immanence in the world. In other mystical texts the process of creation was thought to involve divine manipulation of the Hebrew alphabet. There were even conjectures in which preceding worlds were destroyed as a prelude to the creation of this one.

Varieties of "Nothing"

From such examples, given by both Rabbi Fox and Professor Cohn-Sherbok, it becomes clear that the concept of creation *ex nihilo* has neither a transparent nor univocal meaning. There is nothing less empty of interest than nothing! This has become clear in modern debates concerning the alleged ability of scientific theory to explain how a universe can burst out of a quantum mechanical vacuum. A "nothing" to which apparently pre-existing quantum mechanical laws apply is a very different kind of "nothing" from nothing-at-all and from that envisaged by medieval theologians.[1] It is particularly interesting to learn that, for some Jewish kabbalists, God was the Divine Nothing: that ultimate source, of which nothing could be predicated. The debate concerning other worlds and their significance for Jewish theology is also deeply fascinating, mirroring to some degree the problems that a plurality of worlds has posed for Christian theology. Arguments grounded in religious belief have featured in the cases both for and against extra-terrestrial intelligence, the supposed uniqueness of the Incarnation of God in Christ creating a particular stumbling block for Christians.[2] In Louis Jacobs' rejoinder to Norman Lamm, cited by Cohn-Sherbok, a comparable problem exists for Judaism in that "there are whole worlds for which the Torah, given to humans, can have no meaning".

On such issues, within both Christianity and Judaism, there has been a rich diversity of views. Debate more than resolution has been the norm. Indeed, those who have made a special study of Judaism in relation to science have concluded that within the different Jewish traditions it would be possible to find just about every conceivable position on the relationship between science and religion.[3] With specific reference to the Talmudic rabbis, Noah Efron writes that "it is a simple fact that about anything beyond matters of ritual and law, opinions expressed in the Talmud are typically counterbalanced by conflicting opinions".[4] Astrology, for example, is presented as a true science, but is also described as false, and in some views false for Jews but true for everyone else. It is of course the diversity and debate within each of the Abrahamic faiths that makes it unwise to speak of a Jewish, a Christian or an Islamic view of science. Such essentialist notions fail for many reasons. They demonstrably fail for the medieval period when "most of the great Jewish natural philosophers...were not so much the product of a Muslim ambiance or a Christian ambiance as they were a product of moving from one to the other and often back again", playing a "unique role in mediating between these cultures".[5]

Different views of Genesis

At the heart of Cohn-Sherbok's essay is the contrast between ancient and modern – the contrast between the speculative cosmologies of the past and the authoritative scientific cosmology of today. He shares with Rabbi Fox the conviction that it is not to *Genesis* one should look if one wishes to know how the universe came to be as it is. On close inspection, however, their respective views might not quite coalesce. In which case we have three opinions!

It would be possible to infer from Cohn-Sherbok's account that no value whatever resides in the *Genesis* creation narratives. The "archaic nature" of biblical speculation concerning the beginning of things leads to the conclusion that it is "nothing more than mystical speculation based on unfounded religious presuppositions". Consequently, modern Jews should allow that an ancient, unsophisticated and erroneous view has been superseded by, and must be replaced by, modern science. From Rabbi Fox's account I sense that he would agree that attempts to harmonize the *Genesis* text with modern scientific paradigms are misguided. It is interesting to note that, as early as 1860 in Britain, exegetical attempts to harmonize *Genesis* with geology were already the subject of forceful critique. Among Christian theologians, however, the rejection of the harmonization programme did not entail the conclusion that the creation narratives were to be abandoned as valueless. On the contrary, as the Oxford historian of religion, J. Estlin Carpenter put it, "the true value of the Bible has been enhanced. We have ceased to ask of it what it cannot give us; we cherish all the more highly what it can".[6] For Rabbi Fox, there is clearly still much to cherish once the language of *Genesis* is interpreted as poetry rather than as primitive but false science. There remain fundamental respects in which its early chapters express insight into the nature of God, the nature of human destiny and the relationship between God and humankind.

Referring to the clash between the scientific and the biblical views of creation as he experienced it early in his education, Cohn-Sherbok states that the claim that God was the creator of the universe was not itself compromised and "seemed entirely believable". My question is whether we are to assume that, in recommending the replacement of the biblical with the scientific cosmology, he is now tacitly distancing himself from God-talk altogether. Is the metaphysical belief in the ontological dependence of the universe on a transcendent Creator, which many theologians would still see as compatible with science and which Cohn-Sherbok himself describes as of supreme importance for Reform Judaism, what he has in mind when he refers to the "unfounded religious presuppositions" that underlay the ancient speculations? If it is not, it would be interesting to identify the precise content of these ulterior, defective assumptions.

The Rationality of Creation

As historians of science are aware, there is a certain irony in the antithesis between the biblical account of creation and the conclusions of modern science. This is because belief in a rational Creator and an intelligible, ordered creation provided a resource in the early modern period for the legitimization of scientific activity. The study of nature's regularities, expressed mathematically as physical *laws*, the justification of experimental methods as the most appropriate for discovering the contingencies in creation that flowed from divine freedom, and a commitment to the unity of nature grounded in a robust monotheism, allowed links to be forged between scientific endeavour and the Abrahamic faiths.[7] The metaphor of divine kingship, to which Fox refers, could add special weight to the image of divine legislation for the natural world. Within Judaism the example of Maimonides was of great importance, as Fox and Cohn-Sherbok both indicate. This was because he gave to natural philosophy a carefully qualified but definite role in the apprehension of God's activity, while at the same time granting it autonomy as a field of enquiry. The degree to which the Abrahamic faiths differed in their propensities to encourage the study of creation is currently a hot topic and a complex one because of the contingencies of time and place. What has become clear is that we must expand the range of questions routinely asked. As Geoffrey Cantor has argued in his study of *Quakers, Jews and Science*, we must ask of religious communities whether they felt threatened by science, whether the sciences (and if so which) were to be taught, whether their members enjoyed careers in science or joined scientific societies. How were scientific ideas deployed in local religious contexts and how did different religious groups respond to major scientific innovations?[8]

Once the repertoire of questions is enlarged, it is possible to see more clearly that, even where a theological foundation may exist for the justification of scientific research, other considerations may interfere. Focussing on Anglo-Jewish communities, Cantor has stressed the negative consequences of their socio-political marginality. Whereas there was self-confidence, for example, about Quaker independence that sprang from a considered rationalization of their dissent, Jewish communities in England experienced a different kind of insularity, born of insecurity. This had the consequence that among both Sephardic and Ashkenazi Jews, a striving for social and economic advancement usually took priority over forms of education that might have exposed them to a culture of science. In several European contexts, Jewish leaders would occasionally be heard giving a low priority to scientific endeavour, not because it was inherently bad but because it was seen to dominate the interests of those who embraced it, diverting attention from Talmud.[9] There was something of a parallel in seventeenth-century England where Anglican divines having a propensity for natural history or natural philosophy were discomfited by a clash or perceived clash, not of ideas but of loyalties.[10] There had also been contexts in which science was regarded by Jewish thinkers as the product of an alien Christian or Muslim culture and therefore viewed with suspicion. In the twentieth century the many outstanding contributions to the sciences made by Jews provide a striking counterbalance. Einstein, for one, is well known for aphorisms that imply complementarity between science and religion, as in his remark that science without religion is lame, while religion without science is blind. Even here, however, there is a complication in that Einstein explicitly rejected belief in a personal God; and other Jewish intellectuals who contributed so much, especially to the mathematical and physical sciences, did so as godless Jews.[11]

A question that has proved fascinating to historians is whether particular religious groups have shown a distinctive preference for one kind of science over another. Is it coincidence that astronomy prospered under Islam, that in the seventeenth century Jesuits were at the forefront of work in mathematics and astronomy, that puritan reformers in England favoured applied sciences such as agriculture and medicine in order to reverse the effects of the Fall, that Anglican divines in the eighteenth century fostered a natural history in which divine wisdom could be discerned in the adaptations of flora and fauna? The Quakers studied by Cantor show a particular predilection for botany, reflecting, he suggests, a recreational interest that exposed them directly to the richness and beauty of a created world. The contributions of Jews to the world of science have been extensive and not confined to any one genre, but there is a long lineage of interest in mathematics and physics. Can we say why?

Reactions to Evolution

Taking up the question of receptivity to major scientific innovation, Charles Darwin's theory of evolution has provided a classic test case, not least because it concentrates attention on different meanings of the word 'creation'. Despite a massive literature on the challenge Darwinism posed to Christian sensibilities and doctrine, it was not until 2006 that the first systematic discussion appeared of Jewish responses.[12] As one would have predicted, the subject turns out to be immensely rich and fascinating – not least because of links that have so often been forged between Darwinism and concepts of race. It is a theory that has featured prominently in discussions *of* Judaism *within* Judaism. Its high profile owes much to the recurrent question of Jewish identity and the reactions of Jews to the secular forces of assimilation in the places and cultures where they have lived. A particularly striking study, cited by Cantor, concerns seven nineteenth-century rabbinic responses to Darwin's theory.[13] Of the seven, the only one to reject the transmutation of species outright was not ultra-orthodox but a leading Reform rabbi, Abraham Geiger. One of the lessons to emerge from Cantor's study of the English scene is that Jews sometimes embraced Darwin's theory as a means of attacking those evangelical, conversionist sections of the Christian Church that tended to foster anti-Semitism. In the Darwinism of a celebrated Jewish chemist, Raphael Meldola, Cantor found an unequivocal acceptance of natural selection, which had no equivalent among the Quakers.[14]

The differing responses of the Abrahamic religions to evolutionary theory invite further comparative study because in the resurgence of the fundamentalist or literalist positions that both Fox and Cohn-Sherbok roundly reject there is an interesting twist. In a new genre of Jewish literature several orthodox scientists, mainly physicists, have rejected the separationist position commended by Fox. These latter day defenders of *Genesis* contend, contrary to Cohn-Sherbok, that modern science confirms the authority of Scripture, taken literally, and provides crucial insight into the true meaning of the biblical text. Three of the best known of these apologists are Nathan Aviezer, Gerald Schroeder and Judah Landa. They make an engaging contrast with Christian creationists in the United States. Whereas the 'Christian right' has been largely and resolutely anti-evolution, these recent Jewish commentators find truth in evolution to corroborate the truth in Scripture. Favouring different forms of theistic evolution, they are neither Darwinians nor advocates of a young-earth creationism. The dead-ends and reversals in the history of life are seen by Schroeder not as a problem but as comparable to the journey of the Israelites recorded in the Bible.[15] The apologia bears a resemblance to, but is subtly different from, a pervasive movement within Islamic apologetics, which seeks to demonstrate the supreme and ultimately miraculous authority of the Qu'ran by showing how various verses anticipated the findings of modern science. It is a sad consequence of each of these contrasting forms of religious reaction that they tend to reduce the provenance of religious language to that of natural science, denuding it of its ability to transcend the prosaic.

But to end on a more positive note, I welcome the disclosure in Fox's discussion of a strand of creation theology within Judaism that is sympathetic to human creativity in both science and technology. Taking us back to the vision of Rashi in the tenth century, Fox reminds us of our role as co-creators and of the "moral responsibility and inescapable accountability inherent in the creation story". There is a comparable strand in contemporary Christian theology, given forceful articulation by Philip Hefner in his book *The Human Factor*.[16] It is, however, an engaging question whether this motif, of our being collaborators with the deity in completing the work of creation, might have been more pronounced in Jewish than in Christian piety.

Notes and References

1. Willem Drees, *Religion, Science and Naturalism* (Cambridge: Cambridge University Press, 1996) pp. 266-72.
2. Michael Crowe, *The Extraterrestrial Life Debate 1750-1900: The Idea of a Plurality of Worlds from Kant to Lowell* (Cambridge: Cambridge University Press, 1986).
3. Noah Efron, *Judaism and Science: A Historical Introduction* (London: Greenwood Press, 2006).
4. Noah Efron, "Early Judaism", in John Hedley Brooke and Ronald Numbers, eds., *Science and Religion Around the World* (New York: Oxford University Press, forthcoming).
5. Efron, ref 4.
6. J Estlin Carpenter, *The Bible in the Nineteenth Century* (London: Longmans, 1903) p. 453.
7. For an introduction to a large literature on this point see John Hedley Brooke, *Science and Religion: Some Historical Perspectives* (Cambridge: Cambridge University Press, 1991) pp. 19-33; Peter Harrison, *The Bible, Protestantism and the Rise of Natural Science* (Cambridge: Cambridge University Press, 1998); and

Stephen Gaukroger, *The Emergence of a Scientific Culture* (Oxford: Oxford University Press, 2006) pp.455-509.
8. Geoffrey Cantor, *Quakers, Jews and Science* (Oxford: Oxford University Press, 2005).
9. Efron, ref 4
10. Mordechai Feingold, "Science as a Calling? The Early Modern Dilemma", *Science in Context* **15** (2002) pp. 79-119.
11. Max Jammer, *Einstein and Religion* (Princeton: Princeton University Press, 1999) pp. 121-22.
12. Geoffrey Cantor and Marc Swetlitz, eds, *Jewish Tradition and the Challenge of Darwinism* (Chicago: University of Chicago Press, 2006).
13. Michael Shai Cherry, "Creation, Evolution and Jewish Thought", Ph.D Dissertation (Brandeis University, 2001), ch.2; Cantor and Swetlitz, ref. 12, p. 12.
14. Cantor, ref. 8, pp. 340-45
15. Shai Cherry, "Crisis Management via Biblical Interpretation: Fundamentalism, Modern Orthodoxy, and Genesis", in Cantor and Swetlitz,, ref. 12, pp. 166-87, especially 175-76.
16. Philip Hefner, *The Human Factor: Evolution, Culture, and Religion* (Minneapolis: Fortress Press, 1993); John Hedley Brooke, "Detracting from Divine Power? Religious belief and the Appraisal of New Technologies", in Celia Deane-Drummond and Bronislaw Szerszynski, eds, *Re-ordering Nature*: *Theology, Society and the New Genetics* (London: T & T Clark, 2003) pp. 43-64.

CHAPTER TWELVE

ISLAMIC CONCEPTS OF CREATION AND ENVIRONMENTAL SUSTAINABILITY

MAWIL IZZI DIEN

Dr Mawil Izzi Dien, BA (Baghdad), PhD (Manchester) is Reader in Islamic Studies and Arabic at the University of Wales, Lampeter. His latest books indicate his two main interests; they are:" The Environmental Dimensions of Islam", (Lutterworth, 2000) and "Islamic Law. From historical foundation to contemporary practice" (Edinburgh University Press, 2004).

In this chapter, the original of which was one of the plenary lectures to the 2006 conference, Dr Izzi Dien considers Qur'anic accounts of creation, not cosmologically, as they are treated by Prof Altaie (chaps 2 and 8), but from the starting point of the language used. From this he gradually leads us to examine the Qur'anic stance towards the physical environment in which human beings inhabit the Earth, and demonstrates the powerful challenge to good stewardship which this stance presents.

Introduction

Within Islamic Theology, an intangible topic such as 'creation' can be fraught with ambiguity. The notion of creation lacks clarity itself as it relates both to the creator and the created. Whilst we lack a comprehensive knowledge of the created, insight into the Creator remains even more oblique. According to the Encyclopaedia of Islam "the Muslim tradition tells us that the first verse revealed to Mohammad was Q: 96, 1"[1] This describes God as the one who Created man, out of a (mere) clot of congealed blood….the most Bountiful…Who taught (the use of) the pen…taught man that which he knew not.

He is declared in His transcendent perfections and in His dealings with the world; and every action of the Almighty is the restatement of the mystery which will remain inscrutable, for "the sight cannot perceive Him, while He can perceive the sight" (Q: 6, 103).[2]

Creation and the Language of Qur'an

The Qur'an introduced an innovative vocabulary to the Arabic language, which facilitated the understanding of various concepts once considered as closed areas for the understanding of the human being; including the meaning of God and life itself. Many of these terms are completely new to Arabic in their syntax, but remain within the Arabic semantics and provide clues to the aforementioned mysteries.

Most of the Qur'anic verses relevant to creation were stated in order to establish the presence of the Maker through the signs that "He" has provided. The very fact that God is ambiguous in Islam makes Him "unique" or *Ahad,* since in Islam God is the eternal that was never begotten and there exists nothing equal to Him. The process of creation is described by specific terms which highlight the creation in three stages: Creation *Khalq,* inception *insha',* and synthesis of life or *a'al.*

Khalq is the term in Arabic closest to the English verb "to create". The word often occurs in the Qur'an to designate the *ex nihilo* making of something from nothing.

The Encyclopaedia of Islam (ref. 1) notes that "the noun of the agent, *al-khāliq,* defined by the article, is applied only to God and is one of His Names. According to Lisan al Arab, in the speech of the Arabs *al-khalq* is used to designate the production of something new to a pattern which has not been previously utilised." We could also add that the Qur'anic reference to creation does not indicate a previous creation for elements used in such a process. *Khalq* takes place by the will of God without having to employ the physical rules and principals known to humans.

> To Him is due the primal origin of the heavens and the earth: When He decreeth a matter, He saith to it: "Be," and it is. (Q: 11, 117)

> Verily, when He intends a thing, His Command is, "be", and it is! (Q: 36, 82)

> It is He who created the heavens and the earth in true (proportions): the day He saith, "Be," behold! it is. His word is the truth. His will be the dominion the day the trumpet will be blown. He knoweth the unseen as well as that

which is open. For He is the Wise, well acquainted (with all things). (Q: 6, 73)

Insha' may be translated as "inception". Other Qur'anic terms such as *ansha'a* and *ja'ala* are indicative of secondary divine actions following the creation and denote the inception and development of life. The following verses clearly portray the definition of the verb *ansha'a* to be both the bringing forth and development of that which God has created.

> Say (O Mohammad): Travel in the land and see how He originated creation, then Allah bringeth forth the later growth. Lo! Allah is able to do all things. (Q: 29 20)

> ... verily thy Lord is ample in forgiveness. He knows you well when He brings you out of the earth, and when ye are hidden in your mothers' wombs. Therefore justify not yourselves: He knows best who it is that guards against evil. (Q: 53, 32)

Ja'al or "synthesis", is another key word in the creational vocabulary of the Qur'an.. It appears throughout the Qur'an to denote synthesising the created system and its elements to develop something further. The term most often alludes to the causation of various cosmic phenomena, such as darkness and light:

> Praise be to God who created [*khalaqa*] the heavens and the earth, and made [*ja`ala*] the darkness and the Light... (Q: 5, 1)

The word *ja`ala* is also used in the Qur'an within the context of the creation of human "partners":

> It is He Who created [*khalaqa*] you from a single soul, and made [*ja`ala*] his partner of like nature, in order that he might dwell with her. When they are united, she bears a light burden and carries it about (unnoticed). (Q: 7, 189)

The aforementioned and further verses describing the creation of "partners" do not indicate any hierarchical value. Both men and women are creatures of God and are equal, since they were created – as were all other creatures – by the same Maker.

Creation and Evolution

The question of evolution could be problematic in Islamic theology if creation is taken as a single divine action that occurred at one and the same time. However, the verses quoted previously may help in the understanding of how the notion of evolution could be taken within the Qur'anic view on creation and could support indications that there are other processes of development that take place subsequent to the main action of creation.

The time it took to develop and enhance whatever had been created is not stated specifically in the Qur'an, however many of the verses include "timing sentences", *jumal zamaniyya,* which indicate the process of continuity. This is evident in the usage of *ansh'a,* "to bring forth", as well as in a few terms discussed previously. The possibility of an evolutionary pattern for different stages of creation is referred to by R. Arnaldez in the Encyclopaedia of Islam and is indicative of successive creations:

> It is possible to speak of a creation *ex nihilo* which is primordial and universal, then of succeeding creations which give life to particular beings which occur at different stages of their development. Moreover, the Qur'an alludes to a first beginning of creation. The expression *bada'a al Khalq* does not always refer to an absolute beginning, as in, for example, the case of "He began the creation of man from earth" (Q: 32, 7).

The following verse gives a clue on how light and darkness were "made" after Creation .

> Praise be to God, Who created the heavens and the earth, and made the darkness and the light. Yet those who reject Faith hold (others) as equal, with their Guardian-Lord. (Q: 1, 6)

Accordingly, both light and darkness were not created but brought into being subsequent to the creation. A further clue can be found in the verse relevant to the creation of the sun and moon. The former is described as being made into light and the latter was made to be a reflection of such light.

> It is He Who made the sun to be a shining glory and the moon to be a light (of beauty), and measured out stages for her; that ye might know the number of years and the count (of time). No-wise did Allah create this but in truth and righteousness. (Thus) doth He explain His signs in detail, for those who understand. (Q: 10, 5)

The relationship between all of creation and the earth is encapsulated in the following verse, which uses the same etymological root normally used to describe the growth of plants; perhaps reflecting the cyclical relationship between the biota and the earth:

> And God has caused you to grow as a growth from the earth, [like plants] and afterwards He makes you return thereto, and He will bring you forth again. (Q: 71, 17-18)

Human beings have been placed on the earth to colonise and construct, it.[3] The definition of this term encompasses development, conservation and sustenance of the environment:

> ...It is He Who has produced you from the earth and settled you there... (Q: 10, 61)

An almost exact translation of the modern usage of "environment" is *baww'kum,* and this word is found in the Qur'anic description of the placing of the ancient tribe of Thamud upon the earth:

> ...And gave you habitations [*bawwakum*] in the land ... (Q: 7, 74)

> Behold, thy Lord said to the angels: "I will create a vice-regent on earth." They said: "Wilt Thou place therein one who will make mischief therein and shed blood? whilst we do celebrate Thy praises and glorify Thy holy (name)?" He said: "I know what ye know not." (Q: 2, 30)

Creation and the Environment

In addition to the "nature" of God, there are a number of notions which are perceived within Islamic theology as "incomprehensible to humans"; one such example being the ambiguous nature of God, as stated in the introductory part of this paper. In answer to a question referring to this idea, the reply could be: "Do humans need to know? And if they do, can they, with their limited ability, comprehend the complexity of the answer? Do they possess the faculties to understand what is unlimited? Can creatures who are limited really understand what occurs outside the boundaries of their world?" Moses is depicted in the Qur'an as a great prophet who often gave revelations about human limitations. When Moses asked to see God, He responded:

> God said, "By no means can you see Me (direct). But look at the Mountain." When his Lord manifested His glory on the Mount, He made it as dust, and Moses fell down in a swoon. When he recovered his senses he said: "Glory be to You! To You I turn in repentance, and I am the first to believe." (Q: 7, 143)

Qur'anic Language Regarding the Environment

The Qur'an uses a variety of terms for the environment, which appear to reflect the range of different attributes that ought to be maintained and preserved by humankind. For example, the word *masakin* is used by the Qur'an on several occasions to describe the habitation of all creatures, including that of humans and ants. [4] The root of the term *s.k.n* indicates stillness and comfort. It is often used in Arabic in association with human dwellings, but the Qur'an utilised it to give a meaning that can be easily associated with what is currently termed "animal habitat" (specifically referring to shelters; such as nest sites, burrows etc).

The word earth, *ard* in Arabic, is applied to both the planet and the soil. This word is used a total of 485 times in the Qur'an and many times also in the traditions of Mu.,hammad, the Hadith. The earth is described as the source from which humankind is made and the place where humans end their final journey:

> From the (earth) did We create you, and into it shall We return you, and from it shall We bring you out once again. (Q: 20, 55).

The intimate relationship between humankind and the earth is highlighted by the Qur'an's reference to the earth as a cradle, *mahd*; or as a place for settling, *qarar*.[1] (Q: 11, 64) The Qur'an also states that those who corrupt the earth or its contents will suffer an awful doom (Q: 2, 27), and that the earth belongs only to God and therefore no individual or state has a right to assume that they can do with it what they will. This divine ownership symbolises the earth's freedom from human tyranny; the latter having not only invaded the atmosphere, but also what lies far beneath the surface:

> To Him belongs what is in the heavens and on earth, and all between them, and all beneath the soil. (Q: 20, 6)

Creation and Environment in Qur'anic Theology

Qur'anic theology asserts the presence of a Divine who created every "thing" and who inherently "owns" all that has been created. Let us return to the previously mentioned word *khalq*. According to Arabic lexicology the word also implies, in addition to creation, estimation and calculation.[5] The Universe is thus perceived as an intricate system, connected with both detail and accuracy. Day and night, with their light and shadow; life and death, and how each can be a source of good or evil, are examples given by Qur'anic theology for the numerous "created" systems, un-quantifiable by humans but all carefully calculated by Allah.

The detailed description of creation points to the following central statements:

1. There are systems of creation that complement one another:

> ... in the alternation of the night and the day; in the sailing of the ships through the ocean for the profit of mankind; in the rain which Allah Sends down from the skies, and the life which He gives therewith to an earth that is dead; in the beasts of all kinds that He scatters through the earth; in the change of the winds, and the clouds which they Trail like their slaves between the sky and the earth;- (Here) indeed are Signs for a people that are wise. (Q: 2, 164)

2. There is a purpose for each creation and all have been designated tasks and duties. No part is made without a purpose that fits within the system that God has made. The appreciation of the divine system necessitates a sense of duty and respect, in order to keep such an intricate arrangement safe and complete.

> ... people who celebrate the praises of Allah, standing, sitting, and lying down on their sides, and contemplate the (wonders of) creation in the heavens and the earth, (with the thought): "Our Lord! Not for naught hast Thou created (all) this! Glory to Thee! Give us salvation from the penalty of the Fire. (Q: 3, 191)

3. The processes of life and death are similar in many ways and are seen by Islam as often-repeated symmetrical reflections. Death and life are the ultimate variables of human existence and to understand them is to appreciate the nature of the human role on earth, which was described by the Qur'an as a test:

> Blessed be He in Whose hands is Dominion; and He over all things has power; he who created death and life, that He may try which of you is best in deed... (Q: 67, 1-2)

4. The creation of the dominion that includes the heavens, the earth and whatever lies in between, has taken place in a dimension different from that of humans. The Qur'anic concepts of time and space defy earthly laws. The creation of the heavens and the earth and all that lies between them is described as taking six days to complete (Q: 77, 4), whilst the creation of the earth alone took two (Q: 41, 9). To God, one day may be equal to a thousand years on one occasion (Q: 32, 5), while on another, a day can be equivalent to fifty thousand years (Q: 70, 4).

Environmental Sustainable Development

The concept of "sustainable development" emerged within Western civilisation, as did that of "conservation". They were both wake-up calls to the plight of our planet and reflected the urgency of addressing the frighteningly imminent catastrophe that has been caused by man, one of the youngest species on earth. These concepts represent a response to the major crises caused by the dominance of the material over the spiritual; this seeming to be a development from the Cartesian logic that laid the foundation of a biased scientific paradigm in Western culture. According to S.R. Sterling:

> ... it was a bias of thought over feeling, reason over emotion, fact over value, intellect over intuition, analysis over synthesis, instrumental over intrinsic goals and quantitative over qualitative factors".[6]

The position of Islam towards respect for the planet is not so far removed from that of those who consider the earth to be sacred. Theological convictions may differ, yet if implemented in practice, they can produce the same "purpose". The pillars of faith can be taken as a starting point to understand such a purpose within an environmental connotation.

Accordingly, the testimony of the faith, *shahada*, may be seen not only as a declaration of faith but also as recognition of no power but the power of the system of God. Life, according to the Qur'an; is a form of *shahada* or observation of the physical "open" world, in contrast to the "hidden" and non-physical world of *ghayb*, both of which are ruled by the same One.

> Say, O' God! Creator of heavens and earth! Knower of all that is hidden and all that is open, you will judge between your servants regarding their differences. (Q: 39, 46)

Thus, when planning for conservation, as a practical example, only the environmental public interest *ma·la‚a* should be taken into account, not the interest of companies or individuals in positions of power.

Prayer reflects man's humility before the divine order. The embracing of earth in every prostration symbolises man's position as one creature among many and could be viewed by environmental theologians as part of practice that binds Muslims to the earth and inspires them with love and respect for it. The Qur'an asks:

> Do you not realize that every thing in the heavens and the earth prostrates to God: the sun the moon, the stars, the mountains, the trees, and the animals? (Q: 22, 18)

This verse could also reflect several possible theological concepts, such as the equality of all elements of the environment that are creatures and worshipers of the same Divine and consequently have similar rights of existence and continuity. Worship (*'Ibada* in the Qur'an) includes the notion of man's purposive actions regarding all earthly creatures.

> Messengers eat good things and do good deeds: I am well aware of what you do (Q: 23, 51)

The Hajj (or Hadj) pilgrimage symbolises a festival of sacrifice and love for the natural world. It takes place during prescribed months, and during it no indecent speech, misbehaviour or dispute is allowed. The discipline of *Ihram*, adopted during this period, whereby it is prohibited (among many other things) to kill an animal or cut down a tree, trains people to grant amnesty to the earth and its components:

> Whatever good you do, God is well aware of it. Provide well for yourselves: the best provision [*taqwa*] is to be mindful of God. Always be mindful of me, you who have understanding.(Q: 2, 197)

The Qur'anic emphasis on *taqwa* while discussing Hajj provides an insight into how humans ought to interact not only with each other, but with the entire "family" of creatures that have been created by the same Maker. Although many of the Hajj rituals are not specifically stated in the Qur'an, the tradition of Mohammad (the *Hadith*) provides guidelines for such a ritual. These instructions can be extremely useful to direct Muslims on how to care for nature in an annually sustainable way. Unfortunately in modern materialistic times the opposite seems to be applicable. Hajj seems to pose an environmental problem and not a ritual that inspires respect and awareness for the environment. Quoting Al Riyadh Saudi Newspaper, the Arab environmental monitor stated:

> Experts have warned of an emerging threat of vast environmental pollution at the Holy sites during the Hajj season unless precautionary measures are taken. They urged the authorities to pay attention to the protection of the environment as assiduously as they do to the security, comfort, accommodation and movements of the pilgrims.[7]

Although no direct quote can be found from the Qur'anic verses regarding fasting and environmental sustainability, the essence of this ritual of abstinence can be perceived as a means of teaching self control. Needs and desires are modified so as not to have an adverse effect on the environment. A current major problem is how to encourage universal environmental awareness. As in other Islamic rituals, the concept of *taqwa* lays stress on fasting, since this inspires Muslims to exercise self-control over their mundane desires and physical needs. The Qur'an informs the faithful that the objective of fasting is to foster awareness of God, and this must extend to awareness of man's surroundings, as everything is ruled by the Divine order:

> You who believe, fasting is prescribed for you, as it was prescribed for those before you, so you may be mindful of God (Q: 2, 183)

As in the case of other pillars of the Islamic faith, the prescribed annual charitable donation called *Zakat* is not merely a ritualistic practice, it is a sustained charitable standard based on the benchmark of giving and the application of good to all beings. According to the Qur'an, this was the model of all leading reformers and prophets.

> Those who, when We establish them in the land, keep up the prayer, pay the prescribed alms, command what is right and forbid what is wrong. (Q: 22, 41)

In extension of this, the application of the Qur'anic concept of *ihsan* (meaning "perfection" or "excellence") to the problems of sustainable development and environmental conservation can only bring positive benefit and offer a balancing mechanism to what are often biased and materialistically weighted issues.

The Qur'an repeatedly conveys the message that humanity should only utilise resources when they are available, and never exhaust a resource. Utilisation of a commodity is restricted and the Qur'an cites fruit as an example, although the principle applies to all natural elements:

> It is He who produces both trellised and untrellised Gardens, date palms, crops of diverse flavours, the olive, the pomegranate, alike yet different. So, when they bear fruit, eat some of it, paying what is due on the day of harvest, but do not be wasteful: God does not like wasteful people. (Q: 6. 141)

The Qur'an uses the concept of *Shahada* or "being a witness", not only as a term relevant to the testimony of faith (as previously stated) but as a key term in developing the concept of collective "justice".

> You who believe, uphold Justice and bear witness to God, even if it is against yourselves, your parents or your close relatives; whether the person is rich or poor, God can take care of both (Q: 4, 135)

Muslim scholars often associate this verse with legal testimony but one can observe that the Qur'anic usage of the word relevant to justice is *qawwamın bil qisṭ*. According to some interpreters of Qur'an this term means: *mudawimın 'la al qiyam bil'adl* [8] or the sustainable application of justice. Also one may add that the occurrence of the word *qisṭ* in a definite form could suggest that the justice referred to by the Qur'an is not one that is exclusively practised among humans, but extends to the whole of the earth and its inhabitants. The verse also indicates a non-inclusive social approach to justice. This is particularly useful when we consider the equality of rich and poor nations in the assessment of their environmental responsibilities. While poor countries are expected to conserve the environment, for example by taking measures to halt the destruction of the rainforest or to control birth rates, the rich nations are expected to help them by eradicating poverty. This presents a dilemma that ultimately underpins the prevailing environmental problems. Today there are some rich nations, including Muslim ones, which need reminding of their Qur'anic duty to implement sustainable and just legislation for the maintenance of the environment by aiding and educating the poorer countries.

Islamic Sustainable Practice for Today

The Islamic world is experiencing a conflict between the ideals of the Qur'anic tradition and the practice of industrialization, with all its ecologically unsound baggage. Thus the Muslim world is witnessing a double-edged catastrophe; from global environmental problems and also from the clash of value systems.

Malaysia

Though this problem extends throughout the Muslim world, it is particularly worrying in areas that have a "critical environmental value", such as Malaysia, which contains a third of the world's rain forest. In discussing the environmental problems pertaining to this vital Malaysian biodiversity store[9], Sulayman Kadikon, a native of the area, maintains that:

> One can observe that the loss of natural forests, wetlands and other pristine habitats causes irreversible reductions in the biodiversity store. This is

despite the fact that most of the threatened areas are under the protection of the law. Such a threat to Malaysian biodiversity and natural habitats is caused by the construction of roads, industries, and agriculture which has no respect for the law either due to the difficulty of its implementation, lack of severity or lack of ethical conviction that the environment and its elements are worth protection on account of economic losses and development interests.[10]

Later he adds:

In addition to land development the excessive forest depletion is attributed to: construction of dams, mining, logging and shifting cultivation. A clear example is the development on the Main Range of Peninsular Malaysia which contains the mountain forest habitats which are environmentally important due to their biodiversity and critical ecological functions. Aligned along a north- south direction, these highlands make up the sturdy ridge that runs from the Thai border at Belum Forest Reserve and forms the interior wall down to Bukit Tampin in Negri Sembilan. However, the Highland Resort Highway routed in the late 1990s to connect the three main resorts[11] has seriously destroyed the environmental value of these areas. The potential ecological damage is huge, considering that the route would climb up 25 to 55 degree slopes, sever 21 river basins and bulldoze 85 % of its route through undisturbed mountain forest.[12]

A problem of such magnitude has a bearing not only on the local Malaysian environment but also and more importantly on the entire world. Kadikon suggests an Islamic way to resolve the problem:

The prevention of logging could be introduced into the Malaysian culture by subjecting the area to the protection of Islamic law, which rules the areas surrounding wells and the banks of rivers as ⁻arım or protected zones. Within these zones no one is allowed to develop or construct any building because they are considered as vital for the public interest. The Islamic respect for the environmental elements is no doubt embedded in the religious instruction of Islam which is the basic cultural foundation of the Malaysian Muslim population. This is observed in some ritual practice prevalent among Malaysian Muslim inhabitants, such as economy in the use of water while making prayer ablution or *wudhu*, following the footsteps of the Prophet in doing so. Also the practice of charity to animals is considered important because Islam has enjoined it. Malaysians, particularly those who live in the villages, would not kill a snake if they found it in the jungle because it is a creature similar to them. Perhaps many of them do not know why this practice exists, but only have the explanation that Islam prohibits killing animals that are found in their natural habitats.[13]

Zanzibar

The same Islamic reason that causes the Malaysian villagers to respect nature is evident in other Muslim parts of the world. Adherence to the relevant Qur'anic prescriptions successfully averted a real environmental threat to marine life in Zanzibar. This was observed in an initiative taken by leading Islamic and international environmental groups.[14] The Misali Islands Ethics Project was initiated with the following main objectives:
(a) to publicise the principles of Islamic environmental stewardship
(b) to sensitise marine resource users to the Islamic conservation ethic and
(c) to implement these teachings within the parameters of an integrated conservation and development project, bearing in mind the issues of sustainability.[15]

The direct aim of the initiative was to prevent the local Muslim fishermen from destroying the coral reefs by exploding dynamite as a fishing technique. Their action was a desperate measure to compete with the international trawlers equipped with modern fishing technology that enabled over-fishing and the consequent depletion of local fish stocks. The Qur'anic input was used to influence those local fishermen and, according to the BBC, the result was very encouraging:

> The Qur'an is not widely known as a source of guidance on environmental and conservation issues, but that has not stopped one development organisation in Tanzania from using it to help conserve an island marine park. Religious leaders have been asked to promote conservation messages using the texts of the Qur'an; an approach which has proved a great deal more successful than government regulations ... [16]

According to Fazlun Khalid, chair of The Islamic Foundation for ecology and Environmental Sciences (IFEES):

> There were three workshops based on this teaching resource in November 1999. Two workshops were conducted for local fishermen, local government officials and madrasa (Qur'an school) teachers. The third was held at the Ministry of Agriculture, livestock and Natural Resources and was attended by senior government officials and senior members of the Mufti's Office. These workshops were a great success and representatives of the international NGOs who participated were of the view that the use of the Qur'an as a teaching resource has had the result of sensitizing stakeholders to conservation issues in a matter of days, compared with the poor results achieved over previous years using standard conservation approaches. As a measure of its effectiveness there also have been proposals to use this teaching resource in schools and for creating greater awareness in the adult population.[17]

This project has created much interest in the Muslim world, as reflected in the case of a Tioman Island's marina project in Malaysia [18] and an initiative that the Indonesians ministry of environment is taking in collaboration with IFEES to use the Qur'anic instruction as a basis for public awareness of the environment.[19].

Perhaps the BBC report on the Misali project may be a good note on which to conclude this chapter:

> One local fisherman summarised neatly why the religious message has succeeded where government decrees failed: "It is easy to ignore the government", he said, "but no-one can break God's law".[20]

References

1. L. Gardet, "Allāh." *Encyclopaedia of Islam*. ed. P. Bearman, Th. Bianquis *et al.* (Leiden: Brill, 2007). Also: http://www.brillonline.nl/subscriber/entry?entry=islam COM-0047
2. *Ibid*
3. Mohammad Ali Sabuni, *Safwat al Tafasir* (Beriut, 1980) 2, p. 22.
4. Q: 27, 18; 9, 24; 21, 13
5. Ismail Ibn Hammad Jawhari, *Qamus Al-sihah* (Beriut, 1979) 4, p. 1470.
6. Stephen R. Sterling, *Ethics of Environment and Development* (London: Engel and Engel, 1990) p. 78.
7. *The Arab environmental monitor* (Friday, January 19, 2007): www.arabenvironment.net/archive/2007/1/145775.html.
8. Al Imam, Mohammad Siyuti,*Tafsır wabayan m'a asbab al nuzul lil Siyuti*, Dar al Rashıd, Damascus – ND, 100.
9. Malaysian biodiversity includes:
Over 15,000 species of known flowering plants; 286 species of mammals; over 150,000 species of invertebrates; 1,000 ++ species of butterflies and over 12,000 moths; 4,000 species of marine fishes; 449 species of freshwater fishes; 736 species of birds; 150 species of frogs; 140 snakes, in the grass and other places; 80-odd lizards. From Sulayman Kadikon, PhD Thesis, University of Wales, Lampeter (2004/2005).
10. *Ibid.*
11. The three main resorts are located in Genting Highlands, Fraser's Hill and Cameron Highlands, at a mean altitude of 1,000 metres and traversing a distance of 221 kilometres.
12. Kadikon, ref 9, p. 248.
13. *Ibid*, p. 252.
14. These groups are: *The Islamic Foundation for Ecology and Environmental Sciences (IFEES)* in collaboration with other NGOs such as *CARE International, World Wide fund for Nature (WWF)* and *The Alliance of Religions & Conservation (ARC)*.

15. Islamic Foundation for Ecology and Environmental Sciences: http://ifees.org.uk/index.php? option=com_content & task=view & id=40 & Itemid=55
16. Daniel Dickinson, *BBC News* (Feb. 17, 2005): http://www.arcworld.org/news.asp? page ID=70
17. Islamic Foundation, as ref. 15.
18. Nor Azaruddin Husni Nuruddin, *Paying the price for progress*: http://www.ikim.gov.my/v5/print.php? grp=2 & key=514
19. *Eco Islam* (September 2006) issue no. 2, p. 4.
20. Dickinson, ref 16.

Chapter Thirteen

Can there be a Public Theology of Sustainability? A Response to Mawil Izzi Dien

Celia Deane-Drummond

Professor Celia Deane-Drummond has worked for many years at the interface of biological science and theology, after gaining first degrees (Cambridge, Manchester) and doctorates (Reading, Manchester) in both plant science and theology. She writes prolifically, her most recent books being "Genetics and Christian Ethics" (Cambridge University Press, 2006); "Future Perfect: God, Medicine and Human Identity", edited with Peter Scott (Continuum, 2006) and "Teilhard de Chardin on People and Planet" (Equinox, 2006). She holds a chair in Theology and the Biological Sciences at the University of Chester and is Director of the Centre for Religion and the Biosciences there. She is married with two young children.

In this comment upon Dr Izzi Dien's paper, Prof Deane-Drummond sees close consonance between Islamic and Christian senses of responsibility toward the created order, but stresses that this must be cashed out in secular terms if it is to make political impact. Environmental worth is, however, harder to evaluate by secular criteria than by religious ones.

Sustainability and the created order

I would first of all like to thank Dr Mawil Izzi Dien for highlighting in an important way why it is necessary for those who hold religious views to think seriously about the created order. The practical aspect of humanity relating to the natural world is expressed in secular terms as *sustainable development*. Speaking of creation as such makes complete sense to a religious audience, including all those who share faith in God as Creator, in common with all the Abrahamic faiths. All perceive God as creating by divine fiat, generally considered to have been out of nothing (*ex nihilo*). All can accommodate the idea of evolution by envisaging God's continual involvement in creation, with humanity placed in a position of responsibility over the natural order thus created.

The Islamic idea of human beings as vice-regents has some parallels with the Christian notion of human dominion and naming of the animals, taken from Genesis and understood as human responsibility for creation, rather than domination of it. This idea of human responsibility can be translated into the more secular concept of sustainability. While Dr Izzi Dien believes that the latter concept arose as a reaction to the "frighteningly imminent catastrophe that has been caused by man", I suggest that sustainability understood as integral to the concept of creation makes little sense, or even I would say, no sense, in terms of secular policy-making and planning.

Hence, in order to engage with secular discourse about how the natural world will be treated religious believers need to have a say in the sustainability process as it is understood in *secular* terms if religious insights are to make any difference in public policy. I am not suggesting that we deny faith in God as creator, but rather, try and understand more fully the secular mind-set in order to engage more effectively with particular practices and policies. Of course, we may also wish to encourage those in the religious communities to take the issue more seriously than they have tended to so far, by stressing the religious basis for sustainability, namely, belief in God as Creator, the intrinsic worth of all creation, and humanity as responsible creatures within that creation.

What does "sustainability" mean?

The first question that we need to address is more precisely what we mean by sustainability. Often, in secular discourse, it is couched in terms of the way human society develops and grows, so that, according to one of the earlier definitions by the World Commission on Environment and Development (The Brundland Report): "Sustainable development is development which meets the needs of the present without compromising the ability of future generations to meet their own needs".[1] A much more recent government statement claims quite simply that "Sustainable development is to secure the future".[2] The needs of the present are then defined in economic, social and environmental ways. Often the social and economic goals seem to take priority, so that, ironically perhaps, sustainability language becomes detached from its original inception to integrate human economic growth with the carrying capacity of the earth as a whole.

In addition, the definition is itself open to different interpretations. A strong version emphasises the conservation that was also a central theme in the original Brundland report, so that loss of species limits the options of future generations. But this would be impractical if it were applied literally, so many writers since the classic text of Ward & Dubos[3] have softened the interpretation to allow for some loss (e.g. in biodiversity) as long as there is compensation, even if that compensation means a gain, such as an economic gain, in the human sphere. The question is what loss of biodiversity is acceptable and for what gains? Some want to weaken the definition still further and argue that sustainability means an *increase* in welfare of the current generation providing the needs of future generations are not compromised. Such welfare might include the idea of *quality of life* that might, in turn, include the protection of the land for the sake of those humans who are affected negatively by a species-poor environment.

Others are far more sceptical about the carrying capacity of the environment and whether it can meet these social and economic goals and would press for a far greater degree of constraint, so that all of life is sustained, not just human life. Of course, given the recent public interest in climate change, it is possible that such a view of sustainability will see a comeback, so that weaker versions that stress human benefits alone will no longer find a receptive audience. Climate change is, arguably, the negative outcome of years of industrialised development and lack of attention to the global commons, leading to ever increasing carbon dioxide levels, with negative impacts on global temperatures and weather patterns – the so-called greenhouse effect. Latest figures from the Intergovernmental Panel on Climate Change (IPCC) indicate that problems are going to become increasingly severe, with unpredictable weather patterns, climate extremes, severe drought and flooding, and environmental refugees on an unprecedented scale.[4] The difficulties may eventually lead to an irreversible change, a "tipping point", where the normal self-regulating patterns of the planet are no longer able to absorb the changes in atmospheric gases and temperatures. Michael Northcott, a Christian ethicist who believes such a change is highly likely, warns against complacency among religious believers and secular analysts alike.[5]

However, thus far, consideration of environmental damage and care for the global planet is rarely reflected in the way current policy on sustainability is worked out, which remains utilitarian and instrumental in tone, and anthropocentric, that is, the environment becomes the means to secure the social and economic needs of people. This, astonishingly, is found even in voluntary conservation organisations such as Royal Society for the Protection of Birds.[6] The outcome is that sustainability becomes that which can be measured in a quantifiable way according to public service agreement targets.

Wilfred Beckerman and Joanna Pasek[7] go further in urging that sustainable development is too full of confusions and logical errors to be useful as an economic theory, and it works only as a slogan in as much as it can put environmental issues on the agenda. Of course, this assumes that a stronger version of sustainability, one that includes environmental goods, is understood in such contexts. The alternative, maximum social welfare economic theory, allows for an increase in economic growth followed by a decrease. However, this is a psychologically more difficult theory to accept compared with a steady linear increase as envisaged in sustainable development, even though the overall level of human welfare resulting from it would be more than from sustainable development.

There is therefore a serious issue in a religious endorsement of sustainability if it is unclear what this means, or if it is incoherent from an economic point of view. But perhaps the language of sustainability is here to stay? It does, it seems to me, and as even sceptics such as Beckerman and Pasek admit, allow environmental concerns to be highlighted in policy in a way that perhaps would not be the case if the term did not exist.

What is the environment worth?

Michael Northcott also resists the idea that environmental values, such as climate protection, can be given *any* monetary or economic price tag, for he suggests that this treats the natural world as an object for human use, reinforcing concepts of anthropocentric dominance over the rest of the natural order.[8] In other words, it is philosophically objectionable to treat the environment as an economic category as it cannot be labelled as such, any more than a price tag can be put on the value of human life. He also objects to the so-called "contraction-convergence" principle for the same reason, that is, the idea that those richer countries that generate the most carbon dioxide emissions should contribute economically to those poorer nations that are contributing fewer pollutants per head.

Hence, we are presented with a challenge of whether it is desirable to ascribe economic value to environmental goods. Such labelling may be a convenient measure of ecological damage, but ultimately it fails, as it cannot capture the intrinsic value that many place on the natural world, including those from Christian and Islamic perspectives. Philosophers have used intrinsic value to mean either the value that humans place on non-human creatures, or the value of creatures in and of themselves apart from humans. It is the first meaning that seems to be emphasised here, with an emphasis on equitable distribution between different members of society. Environmental injustice is also an important notion, namely the idea that some sectors of society suffer disproportionately in terms of ecological harms. In consideration of ethical issues in sustainability, it is essential that environmental justice as well as ecological justice is taken seriously.[9]

Of course, if we speak of *ecological justice* we are now back to the difficulty of how this might be measured, or rather, how we will know and protect against cases of ecological *in*justice. How, for example, might we compare the loss of some species over and against some others? In practical, policy terms, we arrive at the difficulty of being caught between a rock and a hard place; while ascribing economic value to the natural order is to be resisted on philosophical and, arguably, religious grounds, positive and practical discernment is left vague and open ended without some more definite attention being given to what this might mean for society, which more often than not, means giving something monetary value. We do not necessarily need to believe that such an economic value is the total of what that creature means to us, any more than a "price" that is often given to the loss of human life in road traffic accidents. Clearly, such loss of life amounts to far more than any monetary price tag, but the economic tag has the advantage of making this meaningful for policy makers and government officials charged with the responsibility of managing the economy and construction of new roads, etc. Hence, while I agree with Northcott that in ideal terms we should resist putting a price tag on environmental goods, it may be necessary as an interim protection measure for practical policy purposes if we are to see changes in policy making that reflect environmental concerns.

It might, of course, be possible to use what other environmentalists have done, and that is, some sort of evolutionary grid so that those species that are more highly evolved, including those that are sentient and conscious, are given a greater degree of protection compared with the less sentient. Unfortunately this will not work when it comes to the contribution of this species to overall ecological and climate stability. For example, those relatively "primitive" (in evolutionary terms) green algal species that are known to be able to trap carbon and become net generators of oxygen. Hence, any grid that reflects human discernment of worth needs to have knowledge of the contribution of that species to local and global environmental stability. Sustainability, if it is to mean anything at all, must mean ways of living that promote overall flourishing for as many species as possible, especially those that are contributing to climate stability. Unfortunately, the lack of knowledge of what species are disappearing, and even lack of identification of existing species, hampers any such global assessment.[10]

Islamic and Christian respect for the natural order

Notwithstanding these issues, the secular environmental organisations that adopt the language of sustainability see religious groups as being another client group that could foster their interests, rather than having something specific and serious to say about sustainability as such.[11] Mawil Izzi Dien shows us that sustainability understood simply as a technocratic process will not do. From an Islamic point of view we must look not just to the future, but also to the past and present; moreover, it is not just about human flourishing, but the well-being of all creatures and forms of life. A religious perspective looks back to the history of human and non-human life in the land, not just present human needs and future goals. Although I might hesitate to attribute the notion of "rights" to creatures, as this phrase has been used in an unfortunate way to promote animal rights in opposition to that of human beings, the idea of broadening the remit of justice so that it is inclusive of the whole created community is a view I share. Moreover, this does not mean that non-humans have moral responsibilities, rather, humans as moral agents have duties to and responsibilities for creatures other than human beings. How do we discern when there is a clash between human economic needs and those of the environment? Here, I suggest, we need the virtue of practical wisdom as well as charity, for wisdom is able to discern what is appropriate in given circumstances, where there is some difficulty in making such decisions.

A Christian approach to sustainability would also emphasise charity towards all creatures in a similar way to that expressed in Islamic texts, a showing of compassion. Such compassion stems from the recognition of God as divine creator of all that exists. It also implies the possibility of intrinsic value understood in terms of value of the creatures in and of themselves. Some Christians would want to go further and argue for an ecocentric or biocentric vision that seeks to compensate for the anthropocentrism that seems to have been so damaging to planet Earth. I am more in favour of the view evident in Izzi Dien's paper, that respect for the natural order does not mean making it equivalent in terms of moral status to human beings. It does mean, however, challenging the secular notion that non-human creatures are simply resources to be managed for human benefit alone. Instead of speaking in terms of natural rights, I prefer to see the natural order as that which expresses natural wisdom, which is also found in human wisdom. Human wisdom expressed in terms of sustainability, is learning to live in tune with the way things are in an ecological sense both now and in the future. Too drastic manicuring and industrial manipulation in the name of regeneration breaks down the respect for the land that is rooted in the history of the experience of human beings with God and God's creation.

Notes and References

1. World Commission on Environment and Development, *Our Common Future: Bruntland Report* (Oxford: University Press, 1987).
2. Department of the Environment, Food and Rural Affairs, *UK Government Sustainable Development Strategy* (London: HMSO, 2005).
3. Barabara Ward and Rene Dubos, *Only One Earth: The Care and Maintenance of a Small Planet* (London: Penguin, 1972).
4. Intergovernmental Panel on Climate Change, *Fourth Assessment Report* (Cambridge: University Press, 2007). For the latest figures see IPCC website, http://www.ipcc.ch/activity/ar.htm
5. Michael Northcott, *The Moral Climate: The Ethics of Climate Change* (London: Darton, Longman and Todd, 2007).
6. John Rodwell, *Forgetting the Land*. M.B. Reckitt Lecture, Mirfield College of the Resurrection (September 7th, 2006).
7. W. Beckerman and J. Pasek in *Justice, Posterity and the Environment* (Oxford: University Press, 2001)
8. Northcott, ref 4.
9. Celia Deane-Drummond, *Ecotheology* (London: Darton, Longman and Todd, to be published 2008).
10. K.J. Gaston and J.I. Spicer, *Biodiversity*, 2nd edn. (Oxford: Blackwell, 2004)
11. Rodwell, ref 5.

Coda

Neil Spurway

Our baker's dozen of contributions has brought us a long way. The scientific background has ranged over some 14 billion years, from the Big Bang – or perhaps even what preceded it – to climate change. The scriptural accounts begin, for all three Abrahamic faiths, with Genesis, chaps 1 and 2, and their precursors in Mesopotamia and Egypt. The subsequent scriptures, and the theologies built on them, diverged substantially, perhaps to a maximum shortly after the death of Mohammad, before reconverging to some extent under the common influence of Greek thought. In the modern era there is further convergence, at least among those thinkers of each faith who engage seriously with science. And this convergence shows at least as strongly in thinking about sustainable development and care for planet Earth as in thinking about cosmology and quantum physics.

Let us end, therefore, with some informal quotations, taken from the three faiths without distinction, which have the common theme that an essential part of worship of the Creator is care for the created world:

The earth is the Lord's, and the fullness thereof.
—*Ps. 24, 1*

The world is green and beautiful and God has appointed you his steward over it.
—*From the Hadith – sayings of Mohammad*

We need to explore without exploiting, want without wasting and produce without polluting.
—*Mona Siddiqui, "Thought for the Day", BBC4, Oct. 18, 2007*

Habitat of Grace.
—*Carolyn King, book title*

INDEX

In this index, only nouns are listed, although some of the text words may be adjectives, e.g. 'Aristotelian' (text) appears here under 'Aristotle' and 'chaotic' under 'chaos'. Also, on a few occasions, e.g. the second reference to 'Anthropic principle', a similar idea is included among the page-references despite the specific word not being used at that point in the text.

Person's names are included only if they carry a total of at least eight lines of subsequent (though not always immediately subsequent) text.

Adam 92, 98-9
al-Ghazali 83-4
ALTAIE, M.B. 13-21, 81-9
animal rights 138
Anselm on God 65, 72
Anthropic principle 25, 86
Aquinas, Thomas 7, 66-9, 71-2, 81-2
Aristotle 67-8, 70, 81, 85
Atkins, Peter 6
atomism, Kalāmic 87
Augustine 30, 63
Barth, Karl 2, 30, 66
Big Bang 6, 24-5, 32, 35, 99
Big crunch/Big rip 36
biodiversity, loss of 137
BONTING, SJOERD 29-38
Brain activity 27-8
BROOKE, JOHN HEDLEY 111-128
Brundland report 136-7
Buckland, William 43-6, 51
Calvin, John 8, 12, 30
catastrophism v. uniformity 43-57
causality 87
Chalmers, Thomas 58-9
Chambers, Robert 46-7
chaos 5, 7, 29, 32-5, 97
chaos-restitution model 59
chaos theology 32-7
Christ, cosmic 35

church councils 30
COHN-SHERBOK, DAN 91-101
climate change 137
clock, cosmic 40
COLYER, PETER 23-8
coral reefs 130
Craig, William L. 32
creation 3, 13, 33, 120-5
creatio continua 26-7, 33-4
creatio ex nihilo 5-6, 16, 24-5, 30-1, 37, 96, 98, 105, 107, 112, 120, 122, 134
creatio nova 24-5
creation stories
    Babylonian 4, 10, 100
    Egyptian 4, 10-1
Creationism 3, 8, 58, 62-3, 109
Cuvier, Georges 42-5, 59-60
Darwin, Charles 46-52, 60-2, 116
'days' of creation 4, 59, 92, 125
DEANE-DRUMMOND, CELIA ... 135-41
development, sustainable 125-131
divine interpositions rejected 60
Drummond, Henry 54, 62
economic theories 138
environment 123-131,137-8
environmental crisis 9-10. 20-1
    Christian guilt for 10, 24-5
eschatology 36-7
evil 31, 33, 62. 85

Index

evolution 26, 46-52, 61-2, 116, 121-2, 134
fall 2
finitude 6
flood 4
FOX, BRIAN 103-9
Friedmann models 19
Gap theory 59
Genesis, Book of, chaps 1-2 ...... 2-3, 17-8, 29-30, 32-4, 37, 58-60, 92, 94, 96, 98-100, 104-5, 113
Gnostics, Gnosticism 5-6, 30
god of the gaps 6
God, personal concept of 82
    difficulty for atheists 84
God the designer 41, 86
God wanting to be known 14
God's changelessness 71-3
God's consciousness 68-70
God's suffering 71-4, 83-5
good, the 67-70, 105
Gosse, Philip 47-8
Gowland lecture 1-2
Gowland, Bill 1-2, 12
great sea creatures 4
Hajj/Hadj 127
harvest v. drought 33
Hawking, Stephen 6, 23-5
Heavens, Qur'anic concept of. 14-18
Hebrew alphabet, letters of 95
homo sapiens 100
Huxley, Thomas Henry 47-9
image of God 11, 18
immanence, divine 62, (85, 87), 106-8, 112
information 34, 36
intelligence, extra-terrestrial 97, 112
Intelligent Design 7-8, 63
intelligibility, ultimate 78-9, 114
intrinsic value 136-8
IZZI DIEN, MAWIL 123-132
J (Yawistic source) 105
Jesus 8, 71, 75
Jewish theologians (mediaeval) 96
Judaism and science 115-7

justice, ecological 139
Kadikon, Sulayman 128-9
Kalām 84, 87
kenosis 31
Khalid, Fazlun 130 Kinglsey, Charles
.... 49, 61
KNIGHT, DAVID 39-55
language, religious v scientific .. 117
life, history of 100
life, natural processes generate ... 97
Logos 34
Luther, Martin 30
Lyell, Charles 44-5, 48-9, 51-2
Maimonides 30, 37, 66, 94, 98, 107, 114
Malaysia 128-9
matter, imperfect 70
Miller, Hugh 59-60
Mohammad 14, 16, 75, 119, 121, 127
Moltmann, Jurgen 31-2, 34
Moore, Aubrey 62
multiverse 86
Mutakallimūn 83, 87-8
mythological cosmology .. 100, 104, 109, 113
mystery 33, 120, 123
natural theology 40
non-linear systems 34
ontological dependence 78, 114
ontological promiscuity 78
Paley, William 40-1
Paris as centre of activity 42-3
Philo 106
Plato 67, 70, 106
Priestly source 104
prime mover 85
'primitive' species, vital 139
purpose for each creation 125
quantum fluctuations 25, 33, 112
quantum states 88
Qur'an 13-21, 30, 32, 120-130
Qur'anic language 120-1, 123-4
rabbinic literature 94, 96, 106
rain forest 129-130
re-creation, principle of 85, 87

relational view of God............ 73-81
Russell, Robert J............................ 6
sabbath 93, 99
scriptural geologists 55, 58-60
sea 33, 36
secular policies............................134
Sedgwick, Adam 46, 61
seven (heavens etc) 4, 7, 14-7
Smith, John Pye............................60
smoke, in Qur'an 16-8
something before creation 105
space-time 4, 24, 83
Spirit, Holy............................... 35-6
SPURWAY, NEIL............... 57-64, 143
sun, fate of............... 19-20, 26, 36-7
sustainability 133-6
stars 8, 99-100
string theory 33
Talmud 97, 101, 106
Temple. Frederick 50
theory of everything 6

Thomist conception of God ... 66-73, 81
Thomson, William.............. 48, 51-2
time, deep/ geological...... 44-52, 59, 62-63
time, God and 72-5, 83, 87-8
time, Kalāmic account.............. 87-8
Torah 94, 97-8
Torrance, Thomas.......................... 5
Trinitarian understanding 3
uncertainty.................................. 83
Universe, age of............................ 5
Universe, cyclic........................... 19
Universe, expansion of................ 18
Universe, fate of................. 18-9, 37
Universe, size of............................ 7
vice-regent on earth 123, 136
WARD, KEITH.......................... 65-79
White, Lynn............................. 9, 20
WILKINSON, DAVID 1-12
Wisdom 7, 106
Zanzibar............................. 129-131